LAURA CHARANZA

UGLY LOVE

A Survivor's Story of Narcissistic Abuse

Disclaimer

The events portrayed in this book are correct to the best of my memory. While this is a work of nonfiction and all the stories in this book are true, some names and other details have been altered for literary effect and to protect the privacy of those involved.

For My Tribe:
Amy, Kim, Sunnie, Tricia and Leah
Rebecca and Ray

CONTENTS

INTRODUCTION

The scars from mental cruelty can be as deep and long-lasting as wounds from punches or slaps but are often not as obvious. In fact, even among women who have experienced violence from a partner, half or more report that the man's emotional abuse is what is causing them the greatest harm.[1]

– Lundy Bancroft, *Why Does He Do That?*
Inside the Minds of Angry and Controlling Men

This is the story of what I thought was my own romantic movie turned horror film. I thought I'd found my soulmate, and then discovered Jekyll and Hyde. This is my truth, and it is a truth that I didn't want to acknowledge for some time. I am not writing this book from the point of view of a psychologist, but from a survivor's first-hand experiences of narcissistic abuse—twice.

Narcissistic abuse is different from physical abuse. The wounds are deeper, yet invisible. There are no bruises, broken bones, or black eyes.

With physical abuse, the victim can point at the perpetrator and say, "YOU hurt ME." With the emotional and verbal abuse inflicted by a narcissist, it happens slowly, usually over a long period of time. It's an insidious, progressive breakdown of self-worth and identity. Sadly, it's evil and intentional. After narcissistic abuse, the victims are left with the belief that something is inherently wrong with them and that they are the sole problem. The narcissist programs the victim to believe that at a natural, organic level, something is so absent in the victim that he or she is not enough, is not worthy of love or respect. Many men and women are victims of narcissistic abuse for over a decade before they realize what's happening. By then, a victim is a shell of what he or she used to be.

> *Narcissistic abuse is different*
> *from physical abuse.*
> *The wounds are deeper,*
> *yet invisible.*

During my years of dealing with narcissistic abuse, my counselor shared a story with me about a mom who gave birth to her son, and when the nurses laid the infant on her chest, the woman screamed, "Get this thing off me!" This boy, now in his teens, has lived every day since trying to win his mother's approval. He hasn't. My counselor told this story to me so that I could understand where the problem originates in narcissism and specifically what it means for its victims. For narcissists, even their own children don't measure up or are held to impossibly high standards. A mother giving birth to a baby should feel an overwhelming sense of unconditional love, not revulsion. The child in this true story was simply born. He didn't do anything to deserve the ugly love he received.

Your experience may not be as momentous or blatant as this one, or maybe it's worse. Regardless, there's a reason you've picked up this book. Mine wasn't a mother who repulsed me, but I did have 46 years with most of them spent as the victim of narcissistic abuse. I can tell you how the damage starts to wear away at your soul. It makes the idea of self-love or true, unconditional love from another human being seem impossible. You feel unworthy, unloved, and simply not enough. You've had that drilled in your head for so many years and heard it so many times, there's a tape recorder playing those critical words over and over inside your mind no matter who you are with or what you are doing.

Until you heal from narcissistic abuse, it's difficult to not attract or be a victim of the next narcissist who comes into your life. I was raised by a parent with narcissistic traits, and then I married a narcissist who was also an emotional and verbal abuser. Don't look at it as your mistake. The nicest, most loving, caring, and intelligent people are duped daily by these masterminds, especially in partnerships or marriages. It's not your fault.

I'm glad you've picked up this book. You've made the first, most important and even life-changing step: recognizing you've been damaged by a narcissist. It is possible to work through your feelings, heal, and decide whether to turn away from or leave the narcissist in your life. I don't want you to live one more day without starting your journey to self-love.

> *Until you heal from narcissistic abuse, it's difficult to not attract or be a victim of the next narcissist who comes into your life.*

Why This Book and Why Now?

Unfortunately (and fortunately), a breakup brought me to my lowest low. A man I loved and thought I would marry after my divorce dropped his façade after eight months, and he left me wondering "What just happened?" This after we had spoken about how many rooms we would need in "our" house and how well our kids got along. It was brutal. He told me he could love me but not my son. Well, I told him, we are a package deal. This deal was off.

I couldn't eat or sleep for days after the breakup. I cried and cried, and I could seldom tell when the tears would come. I recall pulling through a Starbucks drive through in San Antonio, where I had kept it together for a 12-hour work day with a VP at my company. This was the week after we broke up, and by the time I pulled around to the window I was sobbing so hard I couldn't talk. That sweet barista looked at me and said, "Sweetheart, it's going to all be okay." He bought my coffee for me. A simple, kind act from a stranger made the tears fall faster and harder.

On the plane home that night, I realized that my self-esteem and self-love shouldn't be tied this strongly to a man, especially one who wasn't everything I had hoped for in a future husband and role model for my son. I needed to find a way to approach life as some of my closest friends were learning to do: confident, living for God's purpose, and generally just happy.

Through counseling, both through cognitive therapy and spiritual healing, I learned that it was my past experiences with narcissism that were causing me to live this intense pain over and over. Any future breakups would be this brutal because each time I was reliving my futile efforts to win love in both my childhood and my divorce.

So began my journey. Before I go any further, I will say one thing. My mother and I are the closest we have been in this lifetime. I've seen glimpses of her support during and after my divorce. That said, this book looks back at the formative years and her struggles to raise me without a good foundation of her own. So, Mom, know that this book was written to detail the difficult times of my life and yours, not the present time. I wish I could have met your standards.

When I began my healing process, I had to look back and dissect what went wrong to leave me so broken, depressed, and hurt. Looking back, I realized my mother, who I love very much, is a narcissist. From what I've learned about my grandfather, she was raised by one, or a man with enough narcissistic traits to do damage. My mom, it seemed, worked hard every day to win my grandfather's approval. This parental behavior was passed down to her as she became a mother to me and my brother. For us, it was constant turmoil and diligent work to win her love. For me, especially as the same sex child, I never did. If there is any relationship on this earth that should embody unconditional love, it is the love between a parent and child. My mom's love was conditional, based on my looks, emotions, and actions. I was judged for how I looked and what I did, not who I was as a person.

Even my early years were discussed as if I didn't meet her standards and therefore she withheld her love. She told me I was a difficult baby from the beginning. I had colic. I was hard to soothe, and she once recalled her years at home with me as long and lonely. I felt she spoke of the dachshund, Lucinda, with more fondness than she did for me. (Lucinda was a great dog, mind you. She was black and shiny, although she needed a third set of wheels to hold up her long "wiener dog" body.)

Many narcissists tell their victims, "You are too sensitive." The narcissist wants to push the blame on the one feeling hurt, even though the narcissist inflicted the pain. I look back and recall that even as a young girl, I was considered a burden when I displayed my feelings. It was always about how I looked and not how I felt. Apparently, I was a beautiful baby; my family called me "Laura Big Eyes." (For your information, I see my baby pictures and I don't think so. I see drool and chubby cheeks and uncomfortable, smocked dresses.) But, anyway, my point is that through my teenage years, it was looked down upon to cry, show emotion, or let your hair down. Feelings were unacceptable. Appearance was everything.

Then, years later, what do I do? I go and marry a narcissist! He was so charming and sweet, I even overlooked the fact that I would be wife number three! Perhaps I was trying to work out or obtain the elusive, unconditional love that I craved as a child and young woman. This man was verbally and emotionally abusive, with both narcissistic and sociopathic traits. I stayed with him for 16 years, married for 13 of those years.

Today, after a long, arduous, yet rewarding journey, I finally feel as if I have peace, purpose, and love. I am the best version of Laura that has existed. Through a fantastic counselor, a Godly, strong, and even funny Life Coach, and lots of challenging work, I have self-love. I have learned to recognize narcissists and to stay away from them. I've learned why I wanted so badly to win the narcissist's approval. No, I'm not perfect, nor do I want to be. I can laugh at my flaws, embrace my mistakes, and rein in my residual, crazy thoughts of unworthiness and emptiness. For me, it's time to end the generational curse of narcissism—whether becoming one, raising one, or being involved with one.

And you can take action, too. We already know you are strong enough. Someone weak couldn't survive what you have survived. And most importantly, remember: You matter. You are important. You are deeply loved. You are enough.

CHAPTER 1

When It All Blows Up

Nice people don't necessarily fall in love with nice people.

–Jonathan Franzen, *Freedom*

The best way to understand the beginning is to start at the end, which was in 2014.

The plane was somewhere over Kansas. Sweat dripped down my back and pooled at the base of my spine. The air grew heavier. I couldn't breathe. My heart was beating so loud I could hear it and feel it pounding on the walls of my chest. I was scared I was going to black out, and I felt like I would vomit all over the row in front of me. I thought to myself, "I am having a heart attack. I am dying. This is it. At least I won't be worthless anymore."

My seatmate, a sweet, gray-headed lady in her seventies, looked at me and asked, "Are you ok? You don't look so good. I'm going to get you a cold rag." She came back, mopped my face, and held my hand. I swear she was an angel put on that flight to help me. She asked me about my life, my marriage, and my eight-year-old son. I cried and cried and finally started to breathe. She said only a few words to me that flight. It's these I remember most: "You have to simplify your life." The plane landed, I thanked her, retrieved my suitcase, and went to my meeting.

This happened in early February 2014. I was traveling to a mandatory sales meeting in Denver to meet my new boss and sales team at the biotech company where I worked. I later learned I was having a panic attack, although each subsequent attack hit me differently. Panic attacks are sudden periods of intense fear. Many sufferers report symptoms of heart palpitations, sweating, shaking, difficulty breathing, and a feeling that something bad will happen. What triggered this episode? My marriage was at its all-time worst, and I thought it was all my fault. Recent comments by my husband, Shane[1], had added to an already extremely low self-esteem. Mainly his diatribes had led to confusion about what he wanted me to do or be in the marriage. Shane had been complaining for weeks about me traveling to this one-day meeting. Despite his resentment that I worked, he was the first to call my income HIS income and our son "your" son. Interestingly, he traveled considerably more than I did. But, Shane would tell me, "I can't believe you are going to this meeting. It's ridiculous. What will you learn in one day? Don't you know your son needs his mother at home?" The message was that I wasn't allowed to leave him and our young son to fend for themselves.

When I look back now, I have clarity. It was such a double standard. My ex's comments were a way to manipulate me into thinking I was a terrible employee and mom. I offered to quit my job and be that stay-at-home mom he often referenced. Then, he would say things like, "Laura, you can't quit your job. I need the income." (Shane made three times what I made.) So, in addition to working, I was still expected to fill the shoes of a mom who didn't work. How can a woman work a full-time job and be a stay

1 Fictional name

at home mom? It is impossible. I thought Shane loved me because I was working when we met. But, just a few years into our marriage, the target kept moving. The rules kept changing.

There were many other moving targets that appeared early in our marriage. My ex once told me, "I want a Junior League woman during the day and a hooker in the bedroom at night." Huh? I guess he had added "stay at home mom," "business woman," and "female ATM" to his list, too.

Shane often compared me to his first two wives and his girlfriends in between. The messages were mixed and hurtful, and each comment carried a strong implication of "you are not enough." His second ex-wife, he told me, was great at everything. He reminded me that she was always put together, always successful, and a great mom. He told me, "You can't compete with her." Regarding the girlfriend just before me, he often talked about how beautiful she was and that she was great in bed. HE described their love making in detail. He worked hard to erode my confidence and keep me stuck in this marriage. He didn't want the strong Laura to emerge, because she could leave him. By the time he was done, I was a damaged, frail bird. And he had gladly been the one to clip my wings.

> *My ex once told me, "I want a Junior League woman during the day and a hooker in the bedroom at night."*

Several months before my panic attack on the airplane, the verbal and emotional abuse had escalated to the point where I started sleeping upstairs in the guest room.

"Dammit Laura, if you don't open this door I will pick the lock," Shane screamed one night.

3

I cannot remember what he was angry about, but I told him I would call the police if he stepped one foot inside the room. I had already pressed "9-1" and was waiting to press the final "1" if that doorknob turned. It was terrifying. There was no way I was going downstairs to have a conversation like he suggested. His discussions went like this: he would tell me where to sit, and then he would stand over me and yell. I was only allowed to listen.

There wasn't much sleep to be had at this point in my marriage due to the yelling or sleeping in a twin bed with my little one. I'm sure this lack of sleep contributed to the biggest and final panic attack of my marriage. I woke up in the middle of the night and almost called an ambulance to come get me. I was shaking, sweating, nauseous, dizzy, and felt like I couldn't breathe. I was so scared. I knew I couldn't continue like this. I was slowly dying from the stress of this marriage where no one could comprehend what my daily life was like. My husband looked like the epitome of the great Christian man and father. But behind closed doors it was horrific.

That night, I calmed myself down enough to make it through the last few hours before dawn. A neighbor who suffered from panic attacks had told me years before how to handle them. I focused on one point in the ceiling and began counting my breaths. I didn't allow any other thoughts into my mind. Once I was settled down, I dried my sweat off, changed my pajamas, drank some water, and held my little guy tight. (He slept through the whole thing, fortunately).

The next morning, I mentally revisited the terror. I realized then that my marriage had grown from taking a toll on me emotionally to damaging me physically. I knew I had to make a change. My first step was to get away from the abuse as much as I could without moving out. After a year of sleeping in the guest room, I moved into my son's room because it was the only place my husband wouldn't come in and shout at me. He was skilled at telling me that I was a terrible mom, wife, and human being. Shane would tell me that he was the better parent and spouse.

Our worst fights were when he chided me that at least he wanted to work things out. I guess he didn't consider the four counselors we had seen during our marriage. These were four men and women who I had encouraged us to see and had paid for. I did learn from these counselors that a good parent doesn't beat down the other parent emotionally or physically. Also, when you argue with a narcissist, you never win. Don't argue. Walk away.

> *I realized then that my marriage had grown from taking a toll on me emotionally to damaging me physically. I knew I had to make a change.*

When I finally felt like there was no changing my marriage, I began the work to figure out why my husband was the way he was, and what I needed to do. My best friend at the time (she's now deceased, and I miss her every day) told me to read all I could on abuse. I bought a book that was pivotal in my healing. Lundy Bancroft addresses narcissism and abuse in his book, *Why Does He Do That? Inside the Minds of Angry and Controlling Men.* I locked myself in the guest room one night and read it cover to cover. That's when I discovered why I was living a nightmare. I learned about narcissism and psychological abuse.

CHAPTER 2

Different Types of Psychological Abuse

All too often women believe it is a sign of commitment, an expression of love, to endure unkindness or cruelty, to forgive and forget. In actuality, when we love rightly we know that the healthy, loving response to cruelty and abuse is putting ourselves out of harm's way.

– Bell Hooks, *All About Love: New Visions*

There are three types of psychological abusers: narcissists, sociopaths, and psychopaths. For the purpose of this book, we will focus on narcissism, for that's the influence I lived under for 46 years. But first, here's a quick look at the definitions of a sociopath and a psychopath. The first definitions are from the Diagnostic and Statistical Manual of Mental Disorders (DSM), which is for psychology like the Bible is for Christianity.

1. **A sociopath is someone who exemplifies antisocial personality disorder.** Sociopaths **are glib and superficially charming; they are masters of influence and deception. They have no guilt or remorse about exploiting or manipulating other people; winning is the most important thing.** [2]

2. **A psychopath is defined as someone suffering from antisocial personality disorder and who displays a lack of empathy, conscience, and very little regard for authority of the law.**[3]

Often, these terms are used interchangeably, but there are some subtle and not so subtle differences.

Dr. Scott A. Bonn published an article in *Psychology Today*, entitled "How to Tell a Sociopath from a Psychopath."[4] Dr. Bonn notes there are similar traits between the two:

- A disregard for laws and social mores
- A disregard for the rights of others
- A failure to feel remorse or guilt
- A tendency to display violent behavior

Dr. Bonn writes that the key differences are first exposed in his or her demeanor. As per him, "Sociopaths tend to be nervous and easily agitated. They are volatile and prone to emotional outbursts, including fits of rage. They are likely to be uneducated and live on the fringes of society, unable to hold down a steady job or stay in one place for very long. It is difficult but not impossible for sociopaths to form attachments with others."

Psychopaths have a different, more confident and calm demeanor in public. Dr. Bonn hypothesizes, "Psychopaths, on the other hand, are unable to form emotional attachments or feel real empathy with others, although they often have disarming or even charming personalities. Psychopaths are very manipulative and can easily gain people's trust. They learn to mimic emotions, despite their inability to actually feel them, and will appear normal to unsuspecting people. Psychopaths are often well educated and hold steady jobs. Some are so good at manipulation and mimicry that they have families and other long-term relationships without those around them ever suspecting their true nature."

Shannon Thomas is a Licensed Clinical Social Worker who has devoted her Southlake, Texas, practice to counseling those suffering and healing from psychological abuse. In her book *Healing from Hidden Abuse*, Thomas describes the differences between narcissists, sociopaths, and psychopaths with these fictional examples:

A **Narcissist** will run you over and scold you for being in their way. Then they will endlessly complain about how you damaged their car.

A **Sociopath** will run you over, scold you for being in their way, and have a smirk because secretly they get entertainment out of the chaos they created.

A **Psychopath** will go to great lengths and take calculated steps to ensure they run you over, laugh while doing it, and back up to make sure the most damage is done.[5]

Any of the above personalities is dangerous, toxic, manipulative, and can leave you as the shell of the person you once were. The erosion is slow, deliberate, and calculated. And no matter how much you beg for a respite, the abuse doesn't stop. In fact, as long as you are breathing, it gets worse. You are their reason for living. Like the air we breathe, you are their supply.

CHAPTER 3

Narcissistic Abuse and Its Victims

I love the power I have to get you back when you threaten to leave, by throwing a few crumbs your way, and watching how quickly I can talk you into trusting me when I turn on the charm, deceiving you into thinking this time I'll change.

– Leif Beck, "Love from the Perspective of a Narcissist.[6]

What is narcissism? Narcissism comes from Greek mythology and the story of the Greek God Narcissus. Narcissus was the son of Cephissus and the nymph Liriope. Narcissus was a very handsome, beautiful, arrogant, and self-important Greek God who obviously loved himself. Narcissus was going to have a long life unless he recognized himself. Not only did he see his own reflection, he was so enamored by it, he fell in love with himself. And therefore, killed himself.

An easily understood definition of narcissism can be found in the *Encyclopedia Britannica*.[7] Narcissism is described as a pathological self-absorption, first identified as a mental disorder by the British essayist and physician Havelock Ellis in 1898. Narcissism is characterized by an inflated self-image and an addiction to fantasy. These men or woman also display an unusual coolness and composure shaken only when the narcissistic confidence is threatened, and have the tendency to take others for granted or to exploit them. According to Sigmund Freud, narcissism is a normal stage in child development, but it is considered a disorder when it occurs after puberty.

The Diagnostic and Statistical Manual of Mental Disorders (DSM) classifies narcissism as a personality disorder, much like borderline personality disorder or histrionic personality disorder.

The DSM says for a person to be diagnosed as having narcissistic personality disorder, he or she must meet five or more of the following symptoms[8]:

- **Has a grandiose sense of self-importance** (e.g., exaggerates achievements and talents, expects to be recognized as superior without commensurate achievements).

- **Is preoccupied with fantasies of unlimited success, power, brilliance, beauty, or ideal love.**

- **Believes that he or she is "special" and unique** and can only be understood by, or should associate with, other special or high-status people (or institutions).

- **Requires excessive admiration.**

- **Has a very strong sense of entitlement,** e.g., unreasonable expectations of especially favorable treatment or automatic compliance with his or her expectations.

- **Is exploitative of others,** e.g., takes advantage of others to achieve his or her own ends.

- **Lacks empathy**, e.g., is unwilling to recognize or identify with the feelings and needs of others.

- **Is often envious of others** or believes that others are envious of him or her.

- **Regularly shows arrogant, haughty behaviors or attitudes.**

A diagnosis of pathological narcissism—which is a mental health disorder—involves the above criteria. A person must exhibit at least five of the nine traits to be a narcissist. The narcissism personality disorder exists on a spectrum. The more traits you have, the more dysfunction a person exhibits. This means we can have a few narcissistic traits, which we all do and need to survive. For example, you need to have confidence in a job interview or in decisions you make as a parent. However, when several traits are present, this can equate to a full-blown narcissistic personality disorder.[9]

> *The narcissism personality disorder exists on a spectrum. The more traits you have, the more dysfunction a person exhibits.*

According to the largest study ever conducted on personality disorders (PD) by the U.S. National Institutes of Health (NIH), 6.2 percent of the population in the United States has Narcissistic Personality Disorder (NPD) (Stinson et al., 2008).[10] The largest percentage of narcissists are male, although for the purposes of this book I will interchange "he" and "she" when describing narcissistic traits and characteristics. I think the actual number of NPD patients could be much larger, but why would a narcissist go to a therapist to be diagnosed? Unless he is made to do so by a partner, very few narcissists walk through a counselor's door to get help. And sometimes these narcissists are so convincing, they manipulate the therapy sessions so that they look "good and sane" and make their partner look "bad and crazy."

Eddie Brummelman is a developmental psychologist at Stanford University in Palo Alto, California. His research is discussed in a *Psychology Today* article by Rebecca Webber.[11] Brummelman says:

> Narcissistic Personality Disorder is an extreme manifestation of the trait. This disorder can be diagnosed only by a mental health professional and is suspected when a person's narcissistic traits impair his or her daily functioning. The dysfunction might be related to identity or self-direction or cause friction in relationships due to problems with empathy and intimacy. It might also arise from pathological antagonism characterized by grandiosity and attention-seeking.

Brummelman also says, "Narcissism is a continuum, and the disorder sits at the very end." The Narcissistic Personality Inventory or NPI can detect a person's level of narcissism, but additional real-life effects are necessary for a diagnosis of NPD.

Keep in mind that a personality disorder is a pervasive disturbance in a person's ability to manage his or her emotions. These people find it difficult to hold onto a stable sense of self and identity and maintain healthy relationships in work, friendship, and love. They are very rigid and avoid change.

Were my ex and my mom diagnosed? That answer is yes, through attending counseling both times at my insistence. During my marriage, my ex and I saw four different counselors over six or seven years. Each time my ex thought we needed to make a change when he wasn't hearing what he wanted to hear. I foolishly went along. After our divorce, one of the counselors I was still seeing delivered the bad news to me about my ex having

NPD. The counselor's job when we were married was to promote unity, collaboration, and healing of a broken marriage. After a divorce, and my ex severed ties with this counselor, so the therapist told me he had picked up that I had been married to a narcissist. I'll never forget. He said, "Laura, you married a version of your mother."

For my mother, the recognition of narcissistic traits came from my counselor who helped me recover from an eating disorder in high school and college. When I was being treated for anorexia during my freshman year at Southern Methodist University in Dallas, my counselor noticed some of my mother's narcissistic tendencies. Dr. Ray Levy encouraged me to love my mom, but to understand that she wasn't capable of the love I desired. He warned me against trying to meet impossible standards that were set as her child

I believe to this day my eating disorder was a result of trying to have some sort of control over my life and to win my mother's love by being thin. My mother valued thinness. She tried to control everything I did or said. Food restriction, I felt, was my only way to have any independence and still win her love. (I'll discuss more in the healing part of this book.) Dr. Levy says he recognized unhealthy patterns between my mother and myself on the first visit we had as a family, early in 1990. I don't remember that visit, except that I feared my mother, and I was scared for this nice, kind, and calm therapist who asked me to call him "Ray." Mother was livid that we were there in the first place. Dr. Levy recalls how she discredited his statements and fought his opinions and recommendations every step of the way. Dr. Levy graduated from Harvard, where earned his undergraduate degree and subsequent PhD. My mother still thought she knew more. Dr. Levy was obviously brilliant, but he wouldn't be run over. He didn't back down as my mom went after him. I remember her leaving in the middle of the session. She was extremely angry. My father and I stayed until the end. My dad just wanted to get his daughter well. I was near death.

My years as a teenager were tough, but many parents will tell you that raising a teenager is difficult. The most difficult part of dealing with narcissistic abuse came during my marriage. The narcissistic partner, boss, or friend is cold, calculating, manipulative, *and it's all intentional*. In an article written and published online entitled "I Love You From the Perspective of a Narcissist," the author, Leif Beck, says, "I love the power I have to get you back when you threaten to leave, by throwing a few crumbs your way, and watching how quickly I can talk you into trusting me when I turn on the charm, deceiving you into thinking this time I'll change."[12]

I can recall at least a dozen times where my ex stood screaming at me, belittling me, calling me terrible names, and pushing me to the leaving point. I remember clearly an incident in which he was yelling at me, accusing me of being a terrible wife because "his needs weren't being met." At this point, I had been sleeping upstairs in the guest room for about a year. I kept moving emotionally and physically further away from him. I had had enough. I went into the closet and started packing. When I turned around, my ex was on his hands and knees. He had tears rolling down his face.

"Laura, please don't leave," he begged. "You are my everything. I don't mean what I say. I just get angry."

> *The narcissistic partner, boss, or friend is cold, calculating, manipulative, and it's all intentional.*

I turned around and walked into our kitchen. I needed to get away from him for a few minutes and clear my head. Where was this coming from? I had seen the tears before but not the promise to seek help. I had begged him to seek counseling, be kind, and keep our family together. Now, when I am packing to leave, he has an epiphany?

He followed me into the kitchen. "Please, Laura. Give me one more chance. You push my buttons and I get mad."

"Well, I can push some other buttons," I thought. I reached for the phone and called the divorce attorney I had met with a few months earlier.

"Hance Law, how can we help?" the kind voice said on the other end.

My ex then fell to his knees again. "PLEASE Laura One more chance, "he cried. "I'll do anything."

Through tears, I told the man on the other end of the phone that I would call back. Thanks goodness I hadn't given them my name, although I am sure caller ID let them know who the distraught woman was on the other end of the line.

Well, I thought, maybe my ex just *couldn't* change. He seemed to really want to change to keep us together as a family.

I told him, "I found a support group for men who are recovering abusers. They meet each Saturday morning at 10 a.m. in downtown Dallas. I am leaving unless you go."

The next Saturday, with a sliver of hope, I waved goodbye to my ex. "Good luck," I said.

He came home three hours later and said, "These men are different. Most of them hit their wives, too. This doesn't apply to me."

The last sign of hope I had disappeared. I then started preparing mentally, finally, to leave him.

During my research for this book, I learned that it wasn't that he couldn't change. This was all an act, calculated to get me to stay, so he could verbally and emotionally tear me down again, all to build up his own fragile ego and delicate sense of self.

CHAPTER 4

Breaking Down Narcissistic Traits

When I say I love you I mean that I love how hard you work to make me feel like you're everything, that I am the focus of your life, that you want me to be happy, and that I'll never be expected to do the same.

> – Leif Beck, "'I Love You' from the Perspective of a Narcissist," Soulspot.com, 10/17/2017.[13]

The first trait listed in the DSM IV for narcissism deals with the narcissist's feeling and belief that he is the most important one in any relationship. The DSM defines this symptom as follows:

1. **Grandiose sense of self-importance—Exaggerates achievements and talents, expects to be recognized as superior without commensurate achievements.**[14]

The narcissist believes everything and everyone in the world exists to serve or revolve around him. Narcissists expect to be seen and treated as experts in any given field, at any given sport, or in any job, without doing the hard work and diligence it takes to get there. There is a sense of entitlement in a narcissist that infiltrates her personality regarding almost every situation she encounters.

My ex and his needs always came first. He wanted and had the money to buy a new car, but he would complain about buying my son donuts. My son's favorites were $2.16 on most mornings, unless he wanted a chocolate milk, too. But, when I brought up my needs, or the needs of my son, they were dismissed as unimportant or trivial.

> *The narcissist believes everything and everyone in the world exists to serve or revolve around him.*

I saw that my ex-husband, when around acquaintances, would almost always change a conversation to focus back on him. You know that phrase "Enough about me let's talk about you?" I used to joke that his phrase should be, "Enough about me let's talk about me." But it's truly not funny. Most people he encountered didn't like hearing about how much money he made, how many women he had slept with (yes, he said this in front of me quite a few times when we were married!), and how many other women wanted him, except they weren't good enough for him.

Early in our marriage, Shane and I were at dinner with a couple at a local Mexican restaurant. After a few margaritas, Shane started talking about how he and Tim, the other husband at the table, "had a good run" when it came to women before they married. They even discussed some women they had both dated and slept with. Dana, the other wife, looked at me and we both rolled our eyes and tried to joke about it. But I know my face had pain written all over it.

We seldom did things with other couples because of my ex's attitude. He would either bring up inappropriate topics of conversation or criticize something about the people we were out with. It grew to the point where it was just easier to avoid those situations and the embarrassment that came with them. It was miserable because if he wasn't bragging about himself and the conversation didn't revolve around him, he would shut down and contribute nothing. Then, on the way home, he would discuss everything wrong with the people we had spent time with.

These feelings of grandiosity can and do appear in daily interactions. I recently started an online support group, and one of the women who joined vented the other day about her ex and his influence on her three children.

Carrie[2] said, "I get so tired of hearing, 'That's their father. It wouldn't hurt them to spend more time with him.' Yes, the HELL it would!" Carrie said. "This is the same person who lied to the police that my son was abusive. The same person who kicked my autistic son in the back when I wasn't home. The same person who tells his daughter that she needs to lose weight (when she was 9). The same person who tells a 3rd & 7th grader that they won't need the things that they are learning in school and life. The same person who has called me stupid in front of them and told then they were getting a NEW mother. He thinks he knows everything, and the kids think that, too."school in life. The same person who hasn't given them time to get their homework done in 4 years. The same person who has called me stupid in front of them and told them that they were going to have a NEW

2 Fictional name

mother. The same person who has hit his son because he didn't agree with his beliefs (he's a member of a destructive cult). The same person who lies to and on his children. I've overhead them talking to each other about him being a liar. The same person who doesn't spend time with the children when they are with him. This is the condensed version. There's a lot more. earning in school in life. The same person who hasn't given them time to get their homework done in 4 years. The same person who has called me stupid in front of them and told them that they were going to have a NEW mother. The same person who has hit his son because he didn't agree with his beliefs (he's a member of a destructive cult). The same person who lies to and about his children. The same person who doesn't spend time with his children.

Carrie's ex ensnared the children in a web of self-doubt, so the kids believed their dad knew best about school and life in general.

I recall interviewing for my first biotech sales job. I had prepped for days, and subsequently made it through a rigorous interview process. I was one of two asked to come in for a final interview for the position. I remember asking my ex why he didn't offer any supportive comments or encouragement as I prepared for the final, comprehensive panel interview. He said, "Well, you didn't approach things the right way (his way). And I am scared I'll just have to pick you up if you fail."

Narcissists feel such a sense of superiority they cannot put themselves in your shoes, or anyone else's. You gradually stop sharing things with them, such as your fears and doubts and even happiness—because you are met with a blank stare, indifference, or in some cases, outright laughter. The narcissist relishes in ridiculing your thinking and outlook.

One interesting twist to this grandiose way of thinking is that occasionally, a narcissist won't brag about his individual traits if they shine the light on someone else.

> *Narcissists feel such a sense of superiority they cannot put themselves in your shoes, or anyone else's.*

In an article published online for *Psychology Today*, Art Markman, PhD, writes about grandiosity: "Narcissists did not strongly enhance *all* (their) traits, though. Traits that reflect an ability to be part of a community did *not* tend to be enhanced. Narcissists did not think they were more conscientious, fair, likable, or reliable than others thought them to be. This pattern reflects that narcissists inflate their view of themselves to enhance their self-esteem. That means narcissists are focused on having an outsize impact on the world around them. They want others to know them for their individual ability rather than their ability to work with a team. As a result, they are focused mostly on traits that reflect individual leadership and greatness rather than positive traits that would make them better members of a community and team."[15]

Of course. Being a part of a community would mean thinking about someone else's needs above one's own.

Dealing with Grandiosity

Dr. George Simon is an internationally recognized expert on manipulators and other problem characters. He has served as a psychologist to many narcissists and victims through his work, which included time at the Arkansas Department of Corrections. Dr. Simon addresses confronting narcissistic grandiosity on his website, Dr.GeorgeSimon.com.

The way to win,
for me, is no contact.
No conversation.

Dr. Simon mentions that the vulnerable narcissist "really has a low sense of self-esteem. Gently speaking to the narcissist about her behavior and how others perceive it might be the way to approach the sensitive subject."[16]

However, the malignant narcissist will react differently. Dr. Simons writes:

> They aren't compensating for anything or projecting a false image. They act in haughty ways because they truly believe in their own greatness. Such folks neither can conceive of nor do they respect any 'higher power(s).' They harbor a nearly delusional belief about their worth and power. And if you confront that attitude directly, they'll only attack and debase you.

Dr. Simon says confrontation can happen but tread lightly:

> You can effectively confront a grandiose narcissist. But you have to focus on behavior and its consequences. It helps to focus on the distorted thinking predisposing behavior, too. Factual truth can put a dent in these folks' delusions of grandeur. But you can't show animosity when presenting it. Nor can you get anywhere by cutting the grandiose narcissist down to size. That's tempting, but also futile. It only invites their resistance. And it invites them to "dig in their heels" about how they cope. Just stick to the facts. They'll try

to deny them, naturally. But in the end the truth will trump all the lies.

I can tell you that each time I confronted my narcissistic ex-husband, I lost. Three years after our divorce, if we get in an argument, I still "lose" the argument. The way to win, for me, is no contact. No conversation. We can't even text or he blows up my phone. We only email. I keep myself surrounded by other women at sporting or school events for my son. If there's an audience, he won't go after me. If I am alone, I will be attacked. Guaranteed.

2. **Is preoccupied with fantasies of unlimited success, power, brilliance, beauty, or ideal love.**[17]

"I don't care what you think unless it's about me."

– Kurt Cobain

Kurt Cobain speaks the truth here. It must be all about the narcissist. Narcissists consider themselves experts on almost any topic. They often resent others who have success or something that the narcissist covets herself. Narcissists overvalue their own contributions, wondering why another person won that award or made a certain amount of money. There is the ever-present sense of entitlement in a narcissist, even though she hasn't done the work to earn the money or power she craves.

She believes there is a pecking order in society, and she is at the top.

In my experience, the narcissist has always been "better" than any other person to whom he compares himself. She believes there is a pecking order in society, and she is at the top. The comparison game is fun for her because she always wins. The adage, "Comparison is the thief of joy," doesn't apply here. For a narcissist, it could be "Comparison brings me joy, for it shows me that I am better than anyone else."

Also, an example of this self-importance can be seen when someone brags on their employment or job title or position at work. My ex, previously a sales rep for some of the top biotechnology companies, would continually brag about his years of winning the sales award in contests and being the superstar every boss adores. However, he's unemployed right now and has lost three jobs in the last ten years due to his sense of entitlement and superiority at work. After working hard for a few years, Shane wants the accolades but doesn't want to work for them. He criticizes others, including his bosses, which has led to his downfall in at least two of the three recent layoffs. I recall being pregnant with my son, standing by the door to the garage, and hearing my ex rip into his boss at the time. I heard him tell his manager to "*&$! off" when he didn't receive the praise and respect he felt he deserved. A few weeks later Shane was let go with a severance package.

When we were married, my now ex-husband would frequently brag about himself to anyone who would listen. In 2009, I had just landed by first biotechnology sales job. Shane insisted on bringing my new boss over to our home, where he spent two hours showing my boss his toys: A new Range Rover, two motorcycles, a boat, and the list goes on. I was mortified. Keep in mind this was my husband who had just that morning complained that I was wearing a new blouse to work and spending too much of my money on trivial things.

More recently, after our divorce, my ex lost his job again and complained he might not be able to pay child support. In Texas, judges will make a father sell the shirt off his back before they waive child support. A few weeks later, still unemployed, he bought a Ferrari. His needs, especially financial, always came first. But the child support is coming, too, so I don't complain and try to keep my mouth shut.

> *"In normal development, children learn from their parents that they possess an inherent worth that is not attached to performance, looks or status," Dr. Carter says.*

Just a few months ago, I saw another pharmaceutical sales rep who looked familiar when I was flying to Lubbock for work. She used to work with my ex-husband before he was let go for not making his sales calls. She asked me if his stock portfolio was still worth several million dollars. I wasn't sure how to answer this, because Shane always kept his money secret. "Several million dollars?" I thought to myself. My ex had looked at his money as his money and my money as his money (sense of entitlement anyone?). Apparently, one day Shane had opened his e-trade account and reviewed his stock portfolio for his colleagues. He bragged that each time the stock went up a dollar, he would earn tens of thousands of dollars. All I could do was apologize for my ex-husband's actions (I don't know why I apologized. Embarrassment I guess). I did tell this sweet woman to please not judge me by his actions.

Why does the narcissist do this? Again, at the root, it's the fragile sense of self. They are inwardly little boys or girls who want to be validated and admired. They yearn to feel worthy, to feel like enough, and to feel important. Many of these men or women grew up getting their physical needs met, obviously. But, as Dr. Carter writes in his book *Enough About You, Let's Talk About Me*, these children had emotional needs that were ignored.

"In normal development, children learn from their parents that they possess an inherent worth that is not attached to performance, looks or status," Dr. Carter says. "That worth simply is."

Children who aren't emotionally supported by their parents feel like the worth comes and goes. It fluctuates. These children have to make their way through life after learning to focus on the external feeding of their fragile ago, such as popularity, performance, financial success, and looks. Narcissists are preoccupied with the superficial aspects of life like status, weight, and physical beauty, at the expense of committing to deeper values. Therefore, their children who don't measure up in their minds learn to focus on physical attributes as well. It's not who you are but what you have done and what you look like.

A disturbing commonality that I've come across in my research for this book was that many narcissists have a preoccupation with weight and thinness. I had my experiences with being told to never get "fat." One woman who was raised by a narcissistic father, said her father would hug her often and pinch her back fat. Her dad wanted to see if she was gaining weight. To this day, this woman has problems with people hugging her.

My ex was intensely focused on being powerful and admired. Shane thought he was the world's greatest lover and smartest business man. He would even admit that he thought he knew the most about any subject that was being discussed. My ex has criticized coaches, teachers, principals (in one case a PhD), pastors, and CEOs. His favorite phase was "They don't know what they are doing." I remember sitting in church one day, listening to our pastor speak. I couldn't concentrate on the sermon because my ex was ridiculing the pastor's hair, sports coat, and pants. Shane was relentless in finding fault, even with a man of God.

When we would travel to other parts of the world, especially a nice resort in the Caribbean, it was almost unbearable to hear my ex compare himself and me to others around the pool. Shane would comment on, and certainly not compliment, what people were wearing. He would insinuate that others were beneath him, even though they appeared to be financially more well off than we certainly were. One afternoon at a five-star report on Grand Cayman, my ex asked to see the private residences. (There was no way possible we could afford the three- to five-million-dollar price tag of such an island home. But my ex certainly didn't portray that as our reality to the realtor.) He pushed the sleeve up on his shirt to flash his Rolex and talked a big name. When I asked Shane about his visit, he told me the real estate agent was lucky to have such a distinguished gentleman looking at her property. He said she wasn't busy and needed me there. I felt sorry for her.

Even when the focus should rightly be on the rest of the family, my ex didn't let that happen. For example, Shane took paternity leave and spent a week going to have coffee in the morning with his buddies, to eat lunch with the same buddies, and then to happy hour. He would strut through the door at home each evening around seven, armed with diapers, expecting a medal or accolades. It didn't happen. I was recovering from a C-section. Guys—this may be TMI for you—but after a baby you are bleeding, sweating, and hurting, and your breasts are leaking and you are tired, so very tired. Sometimes you just need someone to hold the crying baby so you can shower or go to the bathroom. I remember finally confronting him at the end of his paternity leave.

Tearfully, I asked Shane, "Why weren't you around much this week? You took the time off and I needed you."

Shane responded that he didn't know I had needed him. His said, "Well, Susan (wife number two) knew what she was doing and wanted to do it all on her own. I didn't know. I thought you were the same, and I didn't know you couldn't handle it."

See what he did here? He turned the tables and made it MY fault he was gone all day. Shane insinuated I was incompetent and couldn't properly care for a newborn. He was the dad who was doing what he needed to do (taking twelve hours to get diapers). I had lost all confidence that I was competent, educated, caring, and loving. I needed support. Narcissists can't provide emotional support. They can only suck it from you by demeaning you and putting you down.

3. **Believes that he or she is "special" and unique and can only be understood by, or should associate with, other special or high-status people (or institutions).**

I'm everything that you're not.

— Ahmed Mostafa

If I'm my biggest fan, the only person in the stadium is probably me.

— Craig D. Lounsbrough

The narcissist is typically very critical of others, but reluctant to look through that same lens at himself. They often have conflicts with people who do not meet their approval, yet will tell a significant other that they have "high standards" for who they will associate with. The narcissist is seldom, if ever, at fault. The burden always belongs to someone else. It's their deficiency.

Narcissists are also skilled at playing the "shame game" to place the blame on someone else. When I was growing up, my mom would often say, "Shame on you!" Looking back I can see how worthless that one phrase made me feel. She wasn't calling a certain action or behavior inappropriate, she was calling me, as a person, substandard. I heard her use this phrase with one of my nieces a few years ago, and it broke my heart. My niece had wanted to grab a bite of my mom's lunch, and that obviously didn't go over very well. Mom considered her "shame on you" phrase as part of her way to demand that others meet her expectations, ones that were forever changing and difficult to identify.

I learned to look at any female
through the lens of my
ex-husband.

My ex didn't play the shame game much, unless it was through comparison. Especially when it came to other women, I learned to look at any female through the lens of my ex-husband. Would they be prettier than me in his eyes? I know he likes blondes, will he look at her? Will he say he wants to have sex with her, too?

One evening, our family was out to dinner at a local Maggiano's to celebrate my father's birthday. I saw it coming when a pretty, blonde woman walked by our table. My ex had his eyes on this female as she circled the room heading for the front door. Shane said, "Look at that blonde. She could be your twin. But her jeans fit differently than yours do." My father grew very quiet. It was an inappropriate and hurtful comment, simply for the fact that my ex was watching and critiquing other women while sitting at a family dinner.

This happened often. I was compared to these other women, because Shane felt that he deserved the best. Whether it was how I dressed, cut my hair, or the clothes I wore, I was compared to others, almost always in my presence. My ex wanted to make sure I knew that he could replace me in a heartbeat.

> *Even between the two of us, as husband and wife, I felt like it was a competition.*

Even between the two of us, as husband and wife, I felt like it was a competition. Shane would insinuate that my job was inferior to his because he made more money. Our sex life was inferior to his friends' sex lives, because they discussed it, and well, his friends did things in the bedroom we didn't. Before I understood his manipulation, I would try to change my behaviors, looks, friendships, and even job responsibilities. I wanted to meet his standards and win his elusive love. But again, the rules changed constantly. Because he was special and deserved the best. And I was the one always asked to improve.

My ex also hated for me to have friends who supported me and made me feel like a good sales person, mom, or all around Christian woman. He would belittle my friends and say I always picked friends that were "broken." It didn't "look good" for me or my ex to associate with these people, he would remind me. I would disagree, but he would argue and argue and argue until I ceded to his point and distanced myself from that person. Narcissists are skilled at alienating you from the people who keep you grounded and help you live your truth.

4. Requires excessive admiration.

Confidence is the prize given to the mediocre.

– Robert Hughes

Relational intimacy requires connection. For the narcissist to have even a shallow connection with someone (because any connection a narcissist finds with another person is shallow) there has to be admiration. The narcissist likes to "hold court" and be the center of attention.

My ex and I couldn't go to any events or parties where other men made more money than he did. If we did, it would take weeks for Shane to finish talking about how he could make more money and appear just as good as "John Doe" because he is obviously better. It's just been bad luck for him.

He would often criticize that my brother had everything handed down to him, which was not true at all. My brother supports a family of six on his own and works his tail off to do so. He's smart, capable, and most of all, a Godly man who God continues to bless each and every day with a great wife, great kids, and a great job.

My mother had decades of kids she taught in first grade who still remember "Miss Pam." Even to this day, she's had a former student, now thirty, come up and hug her and say "Hi Miss Pam." She always corrects them and says "It's now DOCTOR Pam or DOCTOR Smith."

I also remember growing up, if we didn't tell her she was the skinniest and prettiest and best mom, she would get extremely down. The home orbited around my mom's feelings and mindset. We tiptoed around her when things were bad. When she was loving and caring, we worked so hard to try to find out how to make that last. It never did. It wasn't good or was "almost" good enough.

Again, this goes back to the narcissistic supply the narcissist needs in order to function in society. It's their protection, armor, and coat against the cold wind of humanity. Being superior trumps all, so the narcissist can never be wrong. You are wrong along with everyone else.

5. Has a very strong sense of entitlement.

An abuser's psychological diagnosis isn't the problem. Their sense of entitlement is.

– Caroline Abbott

Narcissists believe everyone and everything in this world is there to serve her as she sees fit. People exist for her benefit. Rules exist for everyone else, but not her. State or federal laws don't apply to the narcissist. The sense of entitlement is so enormous that the narcissist will take what's his, including someone's money, identity, sanity, and sense of peace.

The best example of entitlement that I remember comes from my ex-husband during the year were engaged, a month before our wedding. I was brought up believing that your spouse is your best friend and that you should be able to trust that person with your feelings, finances, and future. When my ex volunteered to move me out of my one-bedroom apartment to what would be our marital home, I thought "how sweet!" It was less for me to do. Besides, I was out of town that entire week for a mandatory national sales meeting.

> *Narcissists believe everyone and everything in this world is there to serve her as she sees fit.*

My ex did move my belongings. Then, he immediately sold most of them, including my furniture, small appliances, and rugs. He kept the $1200 he made from the sale I didn't authorize, and I never saw the money.

31

While he was moving my things, he found my change jar I used to save vacation money. He kept that, too. Already, what was mine was his. Yet, what was his only belonged to him.

The icing on the cake was after he moved me into his home, four weeks before our wedding date, he asked me to make the house payment. He had KEPT the money from the sale of MY furniture and now he wanted ME to pay the house payment? He told me we would be splitting bills in the future, so I may as well get in the habit now. He also added that I was lucky to live in a "real home" now, after moving from a small, one-bedroom living situation.

When my parents came to Dallas for our wedding, my ex tried to sell the washing machine and dryer back to my FATHER who had bought them as a college graduation gift for me in the first place. My dad was furious. My ex felt entitled to the money.

Finally, one of the greatest demonstrations of my ex's entitlement that still hurts me today was exactly one week before I was to give birth to my son. We had been married three years at this point. I waddled into a local pizza place to meet my ex and his buddy, let's call him John, for dinner. After I hoisted my huge belly and myself up on the stool, my ex looked at his best friend and said, "Hey dude. I forgot to tell you. I paid off MY house today." I was dumbfounded. I started questioning myself about what I had believed marriage to be. My father had taught me marriage was a partnership, and huge decisions like that were discussed as a couple before a final decision was made. My ex and I had bought the house together. Shouldn't I be included in such a monumental decision? Or, if it's designed to be a surprise for me, should such news have come within a private conversation and moment?

It turns out Shane decided to sell stock and pay off our home. I was happy for us, but I also felt insignificant, unappreciated, and unimportant. I felt like a (very large) concubine, my sole purpose being to have his child and remain quiet and subservient.

I did ask my ex about it later, and he made it clear that he had contributed more money to the down payment so he felt it technically was his home. I was more like a guest. He asked, "What did you contribute, Laura?" I should've said your baby growing in my belly, that's what. However, I was seldom quick on my feet with him, because he seemed to always catch me off guard with something I would not expect to come out of a husband's mouth.

I do recall when we went to the title company in 2002 to buy a different home, he asked the title officer, "Why does Laura need to sign the paperwork for the house?"

The officer said, "Well, you two are married, right? And this is your homestead, right? The 'family' home?"

My ex grew very quiet after her statements. I signed my name on the paperwork, too, and then got out of there. After all, I was a working woman who had already been splitting the bills with my husband. We wouldn't have had so much equity in the home had I not been paying bills, funding house payments, and buying groceries. Of course, my ex didn't see it that way.

Exploitive of others.

> Avoid those who seek friends in order to maintain a certain social status or to open doors they would not otherwise be able to approach.
>
> – Paulo Coelho, Manuscript Found in Accra

My ex would be "friends" only with those who could give something back to him. For example, Shane wasn't a great friend to anyone unless he needed them to get something in return. When he lost his job right after

I gave birth to our son, Shane called a friend and asked to borrow a car. This same friend lost a job the next year and Shane sold him our washing machine when his broke. He didn't give it to him. He sold it.

We were at dinner sometime later with this same friend, John[3]. My ex asked John to pay for his share in cash, and then my ex would put the entire meal on his credit card. John forked over the money. My ex put the meal on his credit card and later bragged to me that he had expensed the entire meal as a work expense. Shane told me proudly that he had "gotten us some spending money."

6. **Lacks empathy, e.g., is unwilling to recognize or identify with the feelings and needs of others.**

Your biggest mistake is thinking the other person gets affected or cares about how you feel. You think, your suffering, your feelings, and your pain is felt by the person you're sinking for.
– Himmilicious, Author

In 2005, I had a difficult delivery with our son. As I was in labor and my water broke, my physician realized I had meconium staining. This is when the infant passes his first stool in utero. Meconium is feces. It can be very dangerous because the baby can inhale the meconium at the time of its first breath. The medical term is meconium aspiration.

When my green water broke, my physician said it was time to get me into the operating room quickly. Dr. Madri[4] wanted to perform an emergency C-section because my son's heart rate was dropping. My son needed to come into this world right away.

Shane had complained about being up all night due to our overnight stay in the hospital, so a few minutes before Dr. Madri came in, I sent

3 Fictional name
4 Fictional name

Shane to Starbucks. His complaining about fatigue was wearing me out even more. Never mind that I was the one in labor.

> *My son was here and that was all that mattered. I thought I can endure more pain for this miracle.*

When Shane returned with his coffee, he found the hospital room in a highly active state. The nurses showed him into the ER where I was being prepped for the emergency surgery. The delivery went as well as expected, and my son came out screaming at seven pounds eleven ounces and eighteen inches long.

I'll never forget the nurse bundling that nugget up like a burrito, and then holding him in front of me while the doctor closed my incision. My son was so quiet when we looked at each other as I touched his right cheek.

"Hey buddy," I said. "Welcome to the world, big guy."

My son was here and that was all that mattered. I thought I can endure more pain for this miracle. And in the back of my mind, I hoped that maybe a baby would change my husband and our marriage.

While my son was in the NICU for observation for two days, my ex looked like the great parent. Many friends and family came by to see our new addition. Then, as we were headed home, Shane told me he had ordered a wooden stork for the front yard with our son's name on it. I told Shane that was so nice for him to do, because we were indeed a family of three now. My ex then asked me to pay for the sign out of my personal account when the wooden stork was delivered. I had just had a baby and wanted to be cherished along with our new child. Instead I was paying for my own celebration.

7. Is often envious of others or believes that others are envious of him or her.

Narcissists are consumed with maintaining a shallow false self to others. They're emotionally crippled souls that are addicted to attention. Because of this they use a multitude of games, in order to receive adoration. Sadly, they are the most ungodly of God's creations because they don't show remorse for their actions, take steps to make amends or have empathy for others. They are morally bankrupt.

– Shannon L. Alder

My ex was almost obsessed with people who had more money, bigger homes, and nicer cars than he had. Shane would consistently and almost obsessively talk about one of his friends who was very successful in construction. Shane would discuss at length what his friend owned, from several homes to a yacht, to multiple luxury cars. My ex felt cheated and acted out the role of a victim, wondering why and how he didn't own the same possessions. My ex went as far as asking this friend if he could go into the construction business with him.

As his wife, I grew tired of Shane's obsession with what other people had. I didn't understand why our home and our family weren't enough for him. My son and I clearly fell short somewhere. No matter how hard I tried throughout the marriage, there was always something better or something more Shane wanted.

8. Regularly shows arrogant, haughty behaviors or attitudes.

The biggest challenge after success is shutting up about it.

– Criss Jami

My ex was often the one at parties who people would avoid, my friends told me after my divorce. Shane would make the rounds telling everyone about his new car or boat or some other toy, until the person would walk away. Then he would tell me on the way home that he knew others couldn't believe "that I am so successful" and that they were "jealous of what I have accomplished." He believed strangers or acquaintances really cared and envied his status.

I felt like Shane was in competition with me, too, over something as small as physical fitness. I have worked out religiously since I was in college. It helps me manage my stress, and I feel centered and energized for the day. My favorite things to do are run, lift weights, and attend a modified boot camp class for women. I will enter the occasional half-marathon so I can get a cool T-shirt. My ex was the opposite. He told me once he had a great body and that he didn't need to work out, even for his health. He would look in the mirror and point at his abs and ask me, "How can this happen when I don't ever hit the gym?"

During the last part of our marriage he began to work out more than usual, in addition to his usual yard work. After his first workout at the gym, he came home and, in all seriousness, lifted his shirt and asked me if I "know anyone else who can get a body like this in one day?"

My ex also thought he was above the rules or even law. My ex would steal, lie, and cheat, because the rules didn't apply to him. Speed limits were in place for other drivers. If Shane thought a price for something was ridiculous, he would find a way to "get a deal" or cheat someone out of something. One year he had at least three or four speeding tickets on his desk, and he was completing deferred adjudication forms for all of them. Doing that is against the law, too.

Shane was above all laws and rules.

CHAPTER 5

What Causes Narcissism? Environment vs. Genetics

And we need to know what it is to be human, if we are to avoid becoming narcissists.

– Alexander Lowen, *Narcissism: Denial of the True Self*

Psychologists have researched for decades what causes a person to develop narcissistic personality disorder. Although there are different theories, some psychologists believe it's a combination of several factors, including genetics and environment.

Many psychologists believe that each of us starts life with the potential to become a narcissist. We all have those inborn traits. If we didn't, as infants and toddlers we wouldn't be able to get our needs met. Think of the toddler who smiles and coos to get laughs and admiration, then turns around to throw a full-blown temper tantrum in the grocery store over a cookie. The tot doesn't see past his own needs. Whether the tot is hungry or just wants something sweet or simply wants attention, that is what narcissism does. It puts an extreme focus on the self, and not the self as part of a whole.

Dr. Les Carter is a psychologist who has studied narcissism for 30 years. He practices psychology in Southlake, Texas, and is the author of several books on narcissism. Dr. Carter writes in his book *Enough About You Let's Talk About Me* that none of us begin life without some narcissistic traits. He writes, "No child needs tutoring to learn how to be demanding, obstinate, tuned out, whiny or willful."[18]

Parental boundaries and lessons are what teach children to think outside themselves.

Also, many psychologists agree that narcissists didn't have a level of intimacy in the parent–child relationship needed for healthy emotional growth. Whether it was abandonment physically or emotionally, or both, narcissists didn't witness empathy or true, unconditional love. Dr. Carter writes:

> In order to develop emotional maturity, children need years of satisfying and intimate connections with those around them. Beginning with their relationships with their mother and father, young children need constant messages of affirmation and understanding. If children receive steady messages of love and concern from their primary caregivers, they being to recognize that there is a grand world beyond them, one where their emotions and needs don't always come first.[19]

Forensic psychologists have found that a large percentage of prisoners are narcissists or exhibit other personality disorders. In interviews about an inmate's childhood, one prisoner recalled being four years old and learning to manipulate in order to survive. These people are often neglected as children. As they grow older, they develop traits that cause them to be someone to be reckoned with. They feel they have no choice. It's truly survive or die.

Dr. Carter describes narcissism as the hub of the wheel of other disorders.[20]

(Graphics: Chris Morrow)

Dr. Carter says his research has shown him that narcissism is at the heart of other disorders. He has seen sociopathy, psychopathy, obsessive-compulsive disorder, and histrionic disorder stem from narcissism in patients. The most extreme examples of a psychopath can have their origin in narcissism, such as a Mexican drug lord who orders murders of informants or traffickers by the dozen, with no remorse.

Other extreme examples can include borderline personality disorder (BPD). Patients with BPD can have extremes with moods, self-image, and behavior. These symptoms often result in impulsive actions and problems in relationships. People with borderline personality disorder may experience intense episodes of anger, depression, and anxiety that can last from a few hours to days.

Some forensic psychologists study BPD and its prevalence among inmates in the criminal justice system. One article published in *Corrections Compendium* looked at the prevalence of BPD in prisons. The lead author was Elaine Warden, and she found that emotional instability is a hallmark of BPD. Warden writes that individuals with BPD are at elevated risk for involvement in the criminal justice system. Whereas prevalence rates for BPD in the community are one to two percent, rates among both male and female inmates have been estimated at twelve to thirty percent (Black et al., 2007; Douglas et al., 2007; Jordan et al., 1996; Singleton et al., 1998; Trestman et al., 2007). In fact, the prevalence of BPD in correctional settings is typically higher than in psychiatric in-patient settings (about twenty percent).[21]

Bottom line? These minds and the people that house them can be dangerous. Tread lightly or stay away. And the scariest part is that narcissism is at the root of BPD and other mental illnesses.

If these figures are correct, then most of the population with personally disorders isn't violent. Look at people like my mother. She is an effective and loving teacher and professor, and of course she was far from having a prisoner mentality. However, I can see where the lack of nurture affected my mother in adverse ways.

Mom was brought up in Shreveport, Louisiana, by a strong-willed, intelligent, opinionated father who was an eye surgeon. My grandmother, June, was a sweet, kind, humble stay-at-home mom who did the best she could as the entire home revolved around her husband and his needs. I am not privy to the details of my mother's early childhood years, but I do recall

41

my childhood visits to my grandparents' home. We all tiptoed around my grandfather. We were to never challenge him or sit in his favorite chair. (Of course, that's the first thing my brother and I did as children. We would plop down in that awesome, big, brown plaid chair and eat every single M&M that my grandfather kept in his candy jar. I am sure there were some angry words said about our behavior, although my grandmother kept us sheltered from any outbursts.)

I can only imagine the expectations that were put on my mother growing up with a father as a surgeon and a younger brother who had medical school aspirations. My mom has shared with me that she was overweight in high school and early college. My grandfather would even ask me how much I weighed as I grew up. I can only imagine the stress mom felt to be thin, pretty, intelligent, and successful. She was after all the daughter of a prominent eye surgeon.

Today, I believe she's still trying to live up to such unreasonable expectations. Mom taught first grade for years, and later earned her master's degree. Ten years ago, as she approached 60, she earned her PhD in Early Childhood Education. I've heard her gently correct her former first-grade students (who are now thirty) to call her "Doctor Warner[5]" and not "Miss Pam[6]."

My ex didn't share much about his upbringing, but I can see where and how he developed narcissism. For Shane, it was a way to survive and have a sense of self in a cruel world. My ex was one of three brothers, born to parents who stayed together until my ex was about 8 years old. His mom then worked long hours to pay for raising three boys with no help from their father. Shane seldom talked about his father, who is now deceased, but the two memories he shared were disturbing. His father would lean down to kiss him goodnight, reeking of alcohol. His dad would then rub his scratchy beard on Shane's face. My ex told me he specifically remembers

---

5 Fictional name
6 Fictional name

the smell of alcohol, the scratching on his face, and the sound of his father yelling at his mother.

In both cases, I think my mother and my ex were doing what they could to survive emotionally in such households. My mother was held to extreme standards in a home which revolved around a dictator who exhibited only conditional, unattainable love. My ex was struggling to survive and feel worthy when true, unconditional love from his father was missing, both emotionally and physically. My ex must feel deep inside that he wasn't enough for his father to stay.

Early Experiences with Narcissism

Not only was I a "difficult baby," according to my mother, but my toddler years weren't a piece of cake either. Even as a preschool child, I couldn't show my feelings but I was expected to look good. My mother later told me, "Once you started to walk and grow you were the most beautiful baby. We called you, 'Laura big eyes.' People would stop and stare and say how pretty you were."

I leaned from an early age: Emotions and feelings were bad Appearance was EVERYTHING. If you weren't admired, you were nothing. One of the traits of a narcissist is a grandiose sense of self. Therefore, when a parent sees a child as an extension of herself, and that extension doesn't meet her standards, that's where the problem comes in. We will delve into this narcissistic trait and others in the subsequent chapters.

I recall the responsibility I felt for my mother's happiness during my elementary years. Straight A's? Mom was happy. Looked good and "pretty" and thin? She was happy. If I showed my true feelings, such as anger or sadness, she withheld her comments, compliments, and love. This is when I learned her love was conditional.

One of my earliest memories is when mother dropped me at a local church for "Mother's day out." I am certain she deserved a half day off from the trials and tedium a toddler brings. What I remember most is standing there crying. I don't remember her comfort when she picked me up. I don't remember her saying comforting words when she left. All I remember is watching her drive away and being told to come inside.

Many parents would agree that the teenage years with a daughter can be especially difficult. Mine were, I am sure, in a different way. I tried so hard to earn my mother's love and approval. I was never smart enough, pretty enough, quiet enough, elegant enough, and the list goes on. My mother didn't want me to become my own person. I had questions about sex, so my father handed me a book. I didn't know what a period was, so my dad and my fifth-grade teacher explained it. When I finally got my period around twelve, I came home and cried to mother. I tried hugging her, but she left to go the grocery store and buy feminine supplies. She bought me the thickest maxi pads I had ever seen. She told me I wouldn't use tampons until I had a baby, and she reminded me that sex was bad so I wouldn't use tampons until I was married.

It was about what I did and what I accomplished, not who I was and what I stood for.

Then she posted on our big kitchen calendar a big, red "L" on the days I was supposed to start for the rest of the year. Neighbors and friends would see it when they came in. I was mortified.

During college, I struggled socially. I was a little girl trapped in the body of a young woman. My peers were going to class during the day, but at night, my roommates were partying and having sex and smoking and doing other things college kids do. I was still hearing my mom's voice in my head, critical of these people giving in to human desires, from drinking too much to having sex with boys they wouldn't marry. I wanted to fit in and have fun, but my mother's voice wouldn't let me. I was afraid somehow she would know, and I would lose any chance of having her love me.

My freshman year in college was also when my eating disorder became a major health concern. At 5'6" I got down to 89 pounds. My once-snug jeans fell off my bony frame. Mother always told me that fat people were laughed at and not loved. Fat equals bad. Fat equals unlovable. Fat equals lazy. These remarks would come after the reminder to always put a smile on your face and look your best. For mom, it was all about looks and not feelings. It was about what I did and what I accomplished, not who I was and what I stood for. The eating disorder was a way to control things. Mom told me how to wear my hair (short like Dorothy Hammil) and how to conservatively dress (Laura Ashley anyone?), and that boys wanted only one thing and it wasn't my mind. That's why I restricted what went in my mouth. It was the only thing on this earth I could control. I couldn't control how I dressed, what I said, what I believed, what I did, or how I looked. Otherwise it would mean losing any chance of having mom love me. I wouldn't be worthy of love.

While still undergoing therapy for anorexia during my last two years of college, I earned internships in Little Rock and Dallas in the world of television news. My mother thought I would be a great TV anchor, so she put that idea in my head early on. Mom was correct—I was good. I ended up at a station in a top-ten television market before I was thirty, sometimes sitting on the anchor desk to introduce my pieces. I am not sure what I would've chosen had she not pushed me that way. Mom wanted me to be an anchor because again, that shined the spotlight on her. She could tell her friends about her daughter, the one on television.

Adult Experiences with Narcissism: Meeting
"Mr. Right and Mr. Wrong"

What would I have chosen as a career path? I loved and still enjoy reading fiction and nonfiction literature. I can curl up with a good novel for hours. One of my dreams was to be a college professor surrounded by books in an office with an open-door policy for my students. I would be the professor a student could come see to discuss literature or to talk about life in general. Maybe that's what I would've done…but today, I have no regrets. Either way, what I did for nine years has made me a great speaker, confident under even immense pressure and comfortable around all types of people. Saying a prayer at church or going on a blind date doesn't rattle me due to my journalistic training. (By the way, speaking to a million people on camera is sometimes easier than making conversation with a single man across the table for coffee or wine. I'm just saying…)

In my late twenties, I had clawed my way up through small-market television and accepted a position as a TV reporter at the ABC affiliate in Dallas. The metroplex was ranked number 8 out of 200 television markets due to the high number of viewers in the Dallas/Fort Worth area. It was a big job for a young, courageous, yet naïve woman.

> *I felt like I had followed*
> *all of mom's rules, but I*
> *still wasn't enough.*

During my first years back in Dallas, I had my fair share of dates. And this was before that vast pool of choices in online dating. My mom came to visit me in my one-bedroom apartment, which held really nothing more than a bed and a TV. I was so happy working all hours of the day and night and covering the big news, and I didn't have time to shop for furniture or to concentrate on a social life. But mother thought I needed a man and apparently that I didn't know what I was doing so I could land one. She handed me the book *The Rules*. This self-help manuscript was written to show women how to win the man of their dreams and to "capture the heart of Mr. Right." I have nothing against this book, because there are some great tips for dating inside, but mom handed it to me and said "Maybe this will help you." I felt like she was saying, "Because you certainly aren't good enough to have a man love you on your own merit. Maybe this book can tell you how to dress and act and you will finally land a man." That hurt. I still remember sticking that book in my kitchen junk drawer and throwing it away years later. I felt like I had followed all of mom's rules, but I still wasn't enough.

In my 30s I met the man I wanted to marry, my soulmate, my lover, my best friend—or so I thought. The first several months of our courtship were a whirlwind. I felt like I was in a romantic movie. Here was this nice-looking, charming, successful man who loved *me,* of all people. Our lives were packed with fun. We went on ski trips and beach trips. We attended numerous football games at his alma mater, The University of Texas in Austin. We visited his friends in Houston for weekends of concerts and parties. We attended black tie events. He told me I was his "soul mate" and that he had never met anyone like me before. I thought, "How am I so lucky to have found this amazing man?"

When we met, my ex had been married twice before. He was married for the first time in the 1980s, during college. She divorced him after two years. Two years later, he married his second wife and had a daughter soon after. She filed for divorce from him two years after their marriage. When I delved into his marriages and what happened, he told me that the first marriage fell apart because he felt forced into it. Regarding the second marriage, my ex said that *she* chased *him* and that he couldn't say no. She cooked for him, cleaned for him, had sex with him, whatever he wanted.

He said that marriage broke up when she met someone else on an airplane. Again, he took no part in the disintegration of those marriages. This was a huge red flag that I didn't see or wanted to see. I thought I was in love, special, and starting the best part of my life. I didn't want to stop the fairy tale. I was getting closer to becoming wife number three and no one would stop me.

Several months after that, he introduced me to his daughter from marriage number two. (There fortunately were no children from marriage number one.) We went to Six Flags and rode rides all day. He told me he didn't introduce "just anyone" to his little girl. She was seven at the time. The three of us had a great time. We even rode the log ride and got absolutely soaked. We laughed and laughed, sharing Kettle Korn on the way home.

Later that night my ex said he cleaned out two drawers in his room and wanted me to start keeping some of my things there. I was thrilled. I was being allowed into this special man's life. I couldn't believe two other women had let this man go! I considered myself to be the luckiest woman on the planet.

Fat Ankles

About a year into our relationship, I had just turned thirty and quit my job in television to break into pharmaceutical sales. My ex had connections in pharmaceutical sales, so he helped me land my first job at a "big pharma" company, where I would be a rep who spoke with doctors and left samples of a medication for type 2 diabetes.

I wanted to start a family and marry this great man, and a television job starting at 4 a.m. Wednesday through Sunday didn't allow for much of a dating life. This new sales job did. Unfortunately, that's when the bottom started to fall out. I remember sitting in a Starbuck's in Dallas, and my ex was staring at my ankles. I asked him why he was gawking at my feet and he said, "You can always tell if a woman will be big later in life by the size of her ankles. And yours are big now."

What?!?!? I was so hurt. I had just recently told him about my years in high school and my freshman year in college when I struggled with an eating disorder. I still had minor body image issues. And this man had just pointed out to me that I had big ankles? (They are normal and can carry me in half marathons, I told myself. I kept looking at my ankles. Were they really that big?) Was he serious? Was he joking? Surely he must have forgotten how hard it was for me to let go of my stick-thin, sickly frame and still struggle on the low end of the healthy weight spectrum.

Engagement

A few months after this day in Starbucks, we traveled to Destin, Florida, for my family vacation, arriving a few days early. I knew the night he was going to ask me to marry him because he couldn't keep a secret. Shane said he was going to have a few margaritas to loosen up before we went to dinner because he was so nervous to be doing this for a third time. Then, we went to a gorgeous restaurant overlooking the gulf. Shane may have been nervous, but I was so excited for my future.

After dinner, we drove to another beach and took a cooler with drinks with us. Shane put a blanket out then got down on one knee and asked me to marry him. Of course, I said, "Yes." I couldn't wait to be his wife, and maybe the relationship could go back to the beginning now that he knew he had me forever.

The subtle put-downs continued even after we were engaged. Shane told me that he loved me but that I didn't compare to women he had dated or married before. He would compare me to his previous ex-wives, especially number two.

"Laura, you can't compete," he said more than once. "Everything was perfect with Jane. (Jane is not her real name.) "She won't even go to the mailbox without makeup on. Jane liked (insert any sexual position here) and you won't even try it. You'd really have to step up your game to be in her league."

Are you kidding me?!?!?!?!?! But due to the unfulfilled nature of my relationship with my mother, my subconscious helped me choose another narcissist to try to win that ugly, conditional love. And oh, how I tried.

Even after we were married, I can recall dinners out, when my ex's head would be on a swivel stick as pretty women walked by. Then he would have the audacity to turn to me and compare me to those women. They were complete strangers, but my ex would compare my body, clothes, and hair to those of dozens of other women.

I learned to look at other women through the eyes of my husband. This prepared me for the onslaught of comments and criticisms about me and these strangers. Would he find her more attractive? Would he like her blonde hair better? Would he say something crude like he has before? Shane said a few times that a woman looked like she "would have her ankles pinned behind her ears tonight."

Did my family like him? Mother loved him. She thought he was "perfect "because he as charming and showy as she was. My ex said just the right things to her. However, my sweet dad and Uncle Charlie saw right through my ex from day one, but didn't tell me until my divorce was final 16 years later.

The Rockette Who Rocked My Family

I think the most blatant example I can give is one my father remembers to this day, yet he's too embarrassed to talk about it. This incident occurred during a family trip to New York City on Christmas. My parents wanted to treat my brother's family and mine to the Christmas Show by the Rockettes. It was a delight. At the end of the show, all the children were invited to pose with a Rockette for a professional photo. While we were waiting in line with five kids, apparently my ex taught my seven-year-old some new facial expressions we learned about that evening at my brother's birthday dinner.

"Mom," my son said. "Did you see how tall the Rockette was? Her legs were taller than me! Daddy said he would like to...." And that's where my son made the oral sex gesture with his mouth. He was darting his tongue back and forth.

"What?" I asked my little boy, who repeated the gesture. The table got very quiet.

"I didn't teach him that," my ex said. "He must have learned that somewhere else."

No one in my family believed my ex for a second. There was absolutely no way my seven-year-old would've thought to make that up, along with a comment about the Rockette's long legs. My ex was already teaching my son to disparage women, and I felt powerless to stop it.

CHAPTER 6

Who Are the Narcissist's Victims?

In a narcissist's world you are not their one and only. You are an extension of that person and last place in their mind, while they secure back-up narcissistic supply.

– Shannon L. Alder

Playing the victim role: Manipulator portrays him- or herself as a victim of circumstance or of someone else's behavior in order to gain pity, sympathy or evoke compassion and thereby get something from another. Caring and conscientious people cannot stand to see anyone suffering and the manipulator often finds it easy to play on sympathy to get cooperation.

– George K. Simon, Jr., *In Sheep's Clothing: Understanding and Dealing with Manipulative People*

The narcissist has radar to sense who can feed her narcissistic supply. The term "narcissistic supply" is a concept that was introduced in 1938 by psychologist Otto Fenichel to describe a type of emotional support, admiration, or sustenance needed by a narcissist to survive. This supply comes from a victim, carefully chosen by the narcissist, who can feed her self-esteem. The narcissist is skilled at choosing a man or woman who is extremely kind and quite often an empath. An empath is person who thinks outside of themselves almost constantly. They are very receptive to the emotions of others. Everyone else's needs come before the empath's own. What a perfect target for the narcissist: the victim is the complete opposite, ready to service the narcissist's every need.

Judith Orlean, M.D., is the author of the book *The Empath's Survival Guide*. In her research, she developed what she calls the empathic spectrum, much like the narcissistic spectrum.[22]

It looks like this:

The Empathic Spectrum

Narcissists	Loving, Empathic People	HSPs	Empaths
i	i	i	i

It's interesting that narcissists are on one end of the spectrum and empaths are on the other. Most people typically fall between the loving, empathic people and the highly sensitive persons (HSPs). However, an empath takes sensitivity to another level. Dr. Orlean says empaths can spiritually feel another person's pain or suffering. She says we (I am an empath) energetically internalize the feelings and pain of others—and often have trouble distinguishing someone else's discomfort from our own. Therefore, empaths want to fix what they feel. And narcissists prey on this.

If a victim fights back, the narcissist will often fight back until the narcissist's prey deeply fears standing up for herself.

Whether you are an empath or just a normal, loving person, we will learn in the coming chapters that the narcissist is adept at manipulating almost any victim and any situation to become all about the narcissist. The victim is often left dumbfounded…thinking "What about me?" In a healthy relationship, there is give and take. A healthy relationship means there are discussions about a difference of opinions or beliefs. In a relationship with a narcissist, however, the narcissist is always right. The victim is never acknowledged, and is often even laughed at when she shares her thoughts. The narcissist needs a victim who won't fight back or someone who is a people pleaser. If a victim fights back, the narcissist will often fight back until the narcissist's prey deeply fears standing up for herself.

Narcissists always want their victim to strive for what they consider to be their good standards. But don't get too comfortable with the "good" characterization. Once the narcissist has you meet a certain standard, the benchmark will change. Guaranteed. It's a moving target that you'll never hit. That's how a narcissist keeps you coming back and second guessing yourself. What's acceptable one day is disparaged the next. The narcissist always expects you to "be better" and "do more." And empaths are skilled at going the extra mile to please.

When I was married, our little family often took vacations in Grand Cayman for Thanksgiving week. My son was out of school, and the weather in Texas can be gloomy and cold. The condition I had to meet to book our travel, however, was that I paid for the entire trip. My ex might use airline miles to secure a ticket for him or us, but the hotel and meals overseas would be very expensive. I was told to pay it all. To keep my ex happy, I did.

Grand Cayman is paradise. Seven Mile beach is one of the most beautiful beaches in the world. The sand is as white as sugar and the water is a crystal-clear blue and typically as smooth as glass. On sunny days there is no differentiation of where the sky meets the Caribbean Sea. I could go on and on.

One Thanksgiving morning, my ex and I were walking down the beach as our 6-year-old son ran ahead of us. My ex was very quiet as I chattered along. I asked him, "What's wrong?" He started complaining about being on Seven Mile Beach and said he would rather be in Waco having turkey and dressing with his family. Keep in mind, the trip was his idea. And I had been conned into paying for it. And now he was complaining about being there. I felt like I couldn't win. The target for approval and appreciation had moved again.

Is There a Cure for Narcissism?

When we discover we have fallen in love with a narcissist, married one, or been born to one, the first question we ask is "Can it be cured?" We want the relationship to work. If it can't be happy, we at least want it to be healthy.

Dr. Les Carter examines if and how narcissists can change in his book on narcissism, *Enough about You Let's Talk About Me.* Dr. Carter writes:

> There's very little you can do to persuade a true narcissist to change. By definition, narcissists have a very low ability to incorporate someone else's version of reality because they see themselves as the ultimate keepers of truth. They admit no wrong, or if they ever do admit wrong, it is only a matter of time before they convince themselves they were actually right.[23]

Dr. Carter further explains that narcissists seldom seek treatment on their own. The narcissist is usually given an ultimatum or persuaded to attend therapy. But again, the narcissist uses it to his advantage. "Though they usually have deep histories of anger and broken relationships, they rarely think they are the ones who need help," Dr. Carter writes. "Sometimes they usually come in for a few sessions, but it is usually to prove the other person wrong or persuade me to validate their notions or their manipulation about the other person."[24]

Dr. Carter's comments echo a recurring theme from the psychologists I interviewed for this book. The people seeking help are almost always the victims of these manipulators. They go to counseling to learn about the narcissist and evaluate how to stay healthy in such a relationship, or to leave it altogether.

"Can narcissism be cured?" Dr. Carter asked rhetorically, when we met one Wednesday evening to discuss narcissism in more depth. "The further along the spectrum you go, the more traits you have. So, the answer is no."

> *Therapy can even feed the already inflated ego of the narcissist who is looking for validation for his absurd, unrealistic expectations of his partner.*

My ex and I attended counseling numerous times over our 16 years as a couple. We saw four different counselors over a decade. Each counselor didn't know as much as my ex, or when my ex felt like the counselor sided with me, we had to find another. I can recall watching my ex influence the situation each time we saw a new counselor. He would portray himself as the nice, calm, cool, and collected husband who wants the marriage to work. He would come across as the "good guy" while portraying me as the needy, selfish, never satisfied, and controlling "bad guy." Then, on the way home from counseling, he would often denigrate me for sharing incidents that happened in our marriage that I thought the counselor should know about. For my ex, counseling was about manipulating the counselor, so he could seem like the smart, capable, loving husband, married to a crazy, selfish, and demanding woman. I can tell you from first-hand experience, unless the counselor is very knowledgeable about narcissism and its traits, counseling can be a huge waste of time as a couple. Therapy can even feed the already inflated ego of the narcissist who is looking for validation for his absurd, unrealistic expectations of his partner. My pivotal counseling sessions happened when I went on my own.

There is a small contingent of psychologists who think if narcissism can be fostered in an unhealthy environment, it can be treated.

"For years, personality disorders were thought to be essentially incurable," Dr. Carl Vogel writes in an article entitled "A Field Guide to Narcissism," published in *Psychology Today* on January 1, 2006. "That thinking is changing, but narcissists may be among the hardest cases to crack. An unhappy narcissist generally believes that his main problem is that other people don't treat him as well as he deserves. When you think you're the greatest—and when other people mostly defer to you—why would you want to change?"[25]

One recently published article by Joe Pierre, MD, includes information that supports narcissists changing as they age. Dr. Pierre writes, "Narcissism decreases with age because we are humbled by success and failure over time and our focus gradually shifts from ourselves to our children and grandchildren." [26]

Dr. Pierre has seen narcissists experience crushing defeat as life goes on, after experiencing the inability to achieve perfection. For some, this can lessen narcissistic traits. I have seen my mother change in a few ways. Most importantly, she has learned to keep many of her opinions to herself.

This has happened in the last few months. It has helped more family members choose to spend time with her and invite her to family functions. We love her, but we don't love the criticism.

When I first met Dr. Carter almost a decade ago as a rep calling on his clinical practice, he signed a copy of his book that I referenced above. After he finished, I asked him he could summarize his writing in a sentence. Dr. Carter said he could summarize most narcissistic relationships in one word: "Run."

Since we all know that's not always possible in a parent–child, sibling, or even romantic relationship, let's break these traits down one by one in the coming chapters and learn how to respond to each. Staying or leaving is your choice. Only you know what you can handle. All I can tell you is that there is light and life on the other side.

CHAPTER 7

The Cycle of Abuse

Abusive relationships typically follow a pattern. First, he's the prince charming and you are the princess who deserves to be swept off your feet. It's romantic, and he has never felt this way before. Then, he starts criticizing the little things, or insinuating that you didn't cook or make love as well as an ex-girlfriend or ex-wife. Sometimes he will use silence against you, as if he wants to tell you how badly you performed at a task; but when prodded, he says he's silent because he is such a nice guy. He's passive-aggressive, but you can't quite put your finger on it.

In public, they see Jekyll.
Behind closed doors you
come face to face with Hyde.

Then, there's the isolation. No one can love you like he does. You don't need your friends and family, and besides, he tells you, they are dysfunctional and think you are crazy like he does. But he loves you anyway, so he tells you that you have no choice but to stay with him. Then, when you are empty, soulless, and have no support system, he rages at you. You have nowhere to turn. And even if you did reach out, no one would believe you. In public, they see Jekyll. Behind closed doors you come face to face with Hyde.

This graph illustrates the Cycle of Abuse:

(Graphics: Chris Morrow)

Love Bombing

Love bombing is the loving, exciting stage in the beginning. He is your prince charming and the most romantic man you've ever met. You are his queen and soulmate. He turns on the charm and charisma, gushing about how lucky he is to have found you! He puts you first, above all else. You find yourself falling and falling quickly. It's like an animal snare. You are lured slowly into his waiting trap, following your deepest desire to be fed by praise and protected with his heart. The narcissist has spent years perfecting his hunting skills, and you are his prey. You may have been told that "You are my soulmate," "I've never met anyone like you," and "I feel like we've known each other forever."

> *He told me I was his*
> *soulmate and his first*
> *true love.*

After you open up and share, he tells you a little about his disappointments, but it's all orchestrated around the future. He tells you how he's been a victim with other women who treated him badly. You feel sorry for him and coddle him. You don't ask him to be vulnerable about anything else because he's been just so hurt by an ex or two. I used to think in my Southern drawl, "Well, bless his heart. He hasn't had a real woman love him." You don't know it, but he has. And he has left a trail of victims behind.

My ex love bombed me with tickets to football games, nice dinners out, concerts, flowers, and all of the phrases above. He even went as far as saying in the beginning that he had chosen wrong with his first two wives, until he met me. He told me I was his soulmate and his first true love.

Shane would play more of the victim than badmouth the ex, painting himself as a soulful man who wanted only connection and love.

This love bombing stage lasts different amounts of time, depending on the narcissist and his victim. It could be a few months, or it could last a couple of years. The longest Love Bombing stage I've learned about was from a member of my Facebook group for survivors of narcissistic abuse. Her love bombing lasted about two years. That correlates with what my counselor told me. Dr. Ray Levy in Dallas, Texas, says it takes about two years for the "real" person to come out, if he hasn't already. But, each narcissist is different.

The Tension-Building and Fact-Finding Stage

This is the stage after the love bombing part of the relationship. The narcissist is still courting you, but also trying to learn negative things about you to keep for later use. Perhaps you shared with him a family secret or a story about a difficult time in your life. The narcissist will nod and fake empathy. He may dig slightly for more information. But don't be fooled. The more you share with him, the more ammunition he has for the future.

There were a few times my ex held something over my head that I had shared with him in confidence. For example, I remember sharing the story of my eating disorder with Shane. I opened up with him about the pain of the disease and the difficult recovery. I shared stories about support groups and therapy.

Later that week, in passing conversation with our babysitter, my ex told the sitter about my eating disorder. I was dumbfounded. I asked Shane why he would share that private information with a babysitter, and he told me that I was making a big deal out of something that meant nothing. The problem was, and is, it does mean a great deal to me. It was an embarrassing, difficult period of my life. I didn't want my husband (who is supposed to be my best friend) to share my fight against anorexia with a teenager coming over to watch my toddler. I confronted Shane later that night. The most painful part was that my husband didn't care he had hurt me deeply. He said I was "too sensitive."

The Eruption

This is the stage when the abuser finally releases all his anger and resentment. Once he is ready to explode, the tiniest incident can ignite his rage. As the victim, you may have felt it coming. The tension grows during what should be a routine car ride to church or the grocery store. Or, perhaps you mention you ran into a neighbor of the opposite sex at the drug store, and that person "said the funniest thing." The verbal or physical assault that follows is terrible, like they all are. But you may feel a relief that it's finally over.

In my sixteen years with a narcissistic partner, I can't count the number of eruptions that took place. One outburst especially comes to mind when I think about how something small erupted into something huge—at least for my ex.

It was a gorgeous fall day, and Shane and I were driving down Interstate 35 to watch the Texas Longhorns play in Austin. As we drove through Waco, I looked over and saw a building that used to house the Assistant U.S. Attorney and his staff. I was a television news reporter and anchor in Waco for five years, and I had spent a lot of time in that building interviewing the federal prosecutors about several court cases.

> *Once he is ready to explode, the tiniest incident can ignite his rage.*

I said, "Look Shane, that's where the Assistant U.S. Attorney worked that gave me great news tips and explained the Branch Davidian case to me. Gosh, I do miss that part of the business."

My ex grew so angry it seemed like he was going to drive off the road.

"You had a crush on him, didn't you?" he screamed at me. "I bet you slept with him to get all the news tips. Was it good?"

I was dumbfounded. I was just trying to share with him a part of my life that happened before he knew me.

"No, hon, he was married and he trusted me as a journalist," I told him. "It was one hundred percent professional."

"Yeah, whatever, Laura. You can keep telling yourself that," he replied.

I remember looking out the car door window as we hurled down I- 35. Tears were spilling down my face. I remember thinking, "How much damage will I do to my body if I jump out of the car now and never look back?"

My brother and father both told me that as a woman, if I ever needed them, they would come to the rescue, no questions asked. I almost called my brother when we arrived in Austin. Yet again, I talked myself into staying. That night I prayed that Shane would calm down and we could have a nice night.

Hearts and Flowers Stage

After the abuser has erupted on you, you typically find yourself in a period of calm. You think, "Oh, he's really sorry this time. He just can't control his emotions."

Or, you tell yourself, "He loves me so much that he gets jealous and angry. He doesn't really mean it."

Dr. Lundy Bancroft writes about this stage of the abusive relationship like this:

> He may feel rejuvenated and speak the language of a fresh start, of steering the relationship in a new direction. Of

course there is nothing cathartic for his partner about being the target of his abuse (she feels worse with each cycle) but in the abusers self-centered way he thinks she should feel better now because *he* feels better.[27]

Many times the abuser will apologize. That means he can rattle off an insincere apology such as my ex's favorite, "I am sorry I hurt your feelings." Or an apology like, "I am sorry, but…."

The abuser/narcissist is not sorry for what he said or how he acted. He has probably told you that you did something to set him off. The narcissist almost always shifts the blame back to the victim. It is never going to be the narcissist's fault.

As I mention several times in this book, one of the pivotal resources in my recognition and recovery from narcissistic abuse was Lundy Bancroft's *Why Does He Do That? Inside the Minds of Angry and Controlling Men.* There was a paragraph about abuse that I still read when I feel down and have seen my ex moving on, it seems, without a care in the world. Bancroft writes:

> I have not encountered any case, out of the roughly two thousand men I have worked with, in which one of the abuser's good periods has lasted into the long term, unless the man has also done deep work on his abusive attitudes. Being kind and loving usually just becomes a different approach to control and manipulation and gradually blends back into more overt abuse.[28]

Think about what Bancroft writes. Two thousand men. And he's seen very few cases of true change. I believe it.

I understand how hard this is to hear. Because each time the narcissist abuses us, we want to think his apology afterward is real this time. We want to believe that the kindness and remorse is genuine, and he will change. It's usually all we have left to hold onto. Until the next time. The cycle of abuse, apology, hope, and then abuse again most likely will not end. These illusions of change keep us trapped, sometimes for decades. We stay for hope.

After the incident on the way to a Longhorn game, we arrived in Austin for the afternoon game.

My ex said, "Laura, I am sorry I screamed at you, but when I hear that you had the attention of other men it pushes my buttons. I don't like to think of you with other men."

I thought to myself, well, that's not a real apology, but it's better than nothing. Maybe he's over the anger and we can go on and have a good weekend. So again, optimism surfaced, and my naivety grew. Like many other women before me, I continued to stay for one reason: hope.

CHAPTER 8

The Narcissist's Tactics

Don't judge yourself by what others did to you.

– C. Kennedy, **Ómorphi**

The narcissist has tactics she will use during the different stages of the abuse cycle. These are all difficult to identify when you are in the middle of the abuse cycle, and especially when you are in love. These tactics appear over time, not happening all at once.

Gaslighting

One of the most insidious, yet prevalent, tactics a narcissist uses to manipulate his victim is called "gaslighting." It has the victim believing in her truth, and then gradually the truth is distorted by the narcissist, so that the victim eventually is left with the belief that only her perpetrator can love her and accept her, with her many flaws. The victim is left in a co-dependent relationship with no one else around.

The term "gaslighting" is adopted from the1944 film *Gaslight* starring Ingrid Berman, Charles Boyer, and an 18-year-old Angela Lansbury. The husband and narcissist in the movie, Boyer, does everything in his power to convince his wife, Bergman, that she is crazy. He manipulates her with lies, such as isolating her from people because "it's for her own good." She's left in a home with no one but the maid. Boyer, of course, has already worked on the housekeeper to believe lies about Bergman, so the maid thinks Bergman is crazy, too.

In one part of the movie, Boyer shows Bergman that his pocket watch is missing off its chain. He then produces said watch from Bergman's handbag, convincing her she is crazy and the only person who cares for her and protects her from herself is him. It's maddening to watch.

Leslie Vernick, author of *The Emotionally Destructive Marriage,* calls this crazy-making behavior. Vernick described gaslighting as when "one person demonstrates a pattern of deceiving the other through lying, hiding, pretending, misleading, or twisting information to make something appear other than what it is."[29]

Preston Ni is the author of the book, *How to Successfully Handle Gaslighters and Stop Psychological Bullying.* Dr. Ni has identified seven stages of gaslighting, as follows. These are taken from an article he published in *Psychology Today* on April 2017.[30]

1. **Lie and Exaggerate. The gaslighter creates a negative narrative about the gaslightee ("There's something wrong and inadequate about you"), thereby putting the gaslightee on the defensive.**

"Laura, you think you are all that," said my ex during our marriage. "You can't compete with Leslie (ex-wife number two). She's over the top. You can't compete."

It should have never been a competition. But my ex wanted me to work harder to please him.

"That father is a terrible dad and his kid is wheels off," my ex said about our son's friend. "Why don't you tell them? Someone needs to speak the truth to that dad. I know you are just too nice. If you don't, I will. But I never see him. I know you are all chummy chummy with him."

Me, sarcastically, "Guess it's all my fault the father doesn't know his kid is getting into lots of trouble. Maybe, Shane, you should go set the record straight with him."

2. **Repetition. Like psychological warfare, the falsehoods are repeated constantly in order to stay on the offensive, control the conversation, and dominate the relationship.**

I constantly heard from my ex that I wasn't good enough. Shane would say, "You can't divorce me and live downtown. You can't compete with those twenty-something women."

Again, I didn't know it was a competition.

I interviewed for my second biotech sales job for a great start-up based in Boston. After I had prepped for weeks, my ex wouldn't even wish me good luck because "I might fail."

I later got a big paycheck when our company was sold. "Don't go thinking you are all that now," my ex told me. "I can see you saying, 'I am woman hear me roar.'"

I thought he would be happy for US. My payout could have been a life changer for us as a couple and as a family. When he still degraded me, I knew I was dealing with more than an unsupportive spouse. Yet again, I was dealing with psychological abuse.

3. **Escalate When Challenged. When called on their lies, the gaslighter escalates the dispute by doubling and tripling down on their attacks, refuting substantive evidence with denial, blame, and more false claims (misdirection), sowing doubt and confusion.**

We were on the way to Shane's mom's home for Thanksgiving one November. We had stopped traveling to Grand Cayman for the holiday week as we had done in the past, per my ex's request, as I mentioned earlier. My ex wanted to see his mother and eat turkey and dressing, not spend thanksgiving on a beach trip that he told me to pay for. So guess what? We were going to Waco. My ex complained about that, too. Anyway, we left Dallas for the ninety-minute drive in heavy holiday traffic. We were in my ex-husband's latest acquisition, a brand-new Range Rover. He was tailgating in the left lane in stop-and-go traffic on Interstate 35. We would accelerate to about sixty miles an hour then stop. My seven-year-old was in his booster chair in the back seat watching a movie. I asked my ex to slow down.

Minutes later, the car in front of us slammed on its brakes. My ex reacted quickly, and we didn't hit the car in front of us. But, the man behind us slammed into my ex's prize possession with a loud BANG. I turned around to make sure my son was okay. He said, "What happened mommy?"

My ex instead answered him and said, "I was in a hurry because your mom doesn't want to go to Waco." I was baffled. If anyone wanted to go to Waco it was me. I just wanted my ex to find his elusive happiness and be kind to our family.

Later that evening, in tears, I asked him about his accusation that the car accident was my fault. My husband replied, "I never said that. You must've misheard me. There you go making things up again. Even your father says you make things up. Geez, Laura."

I was left thinking that my rock, my father, was even against me now and thought I was crazy. At that point, I felt like there was nowhere to turn. Even my family thought I was crazy.

Another tactic used by the gaslighter is to enjoy the escalation, and then when you yell back out of anger, to calmly look at you and question your sanity. Dr. Bancroft describes it perfectly in his book, *Why Does He do That? Inside the Minds of Angry and Controlling Men*. When I read this paragraph, every single word resonated with my experience:

YOUR ABUSIVE PARTNER DOESN'T HAVE A PROBLEM WITH HIS ANGER; HE HAS A PROBLEM WITH YOUR ANGER. One of the basic human rights he takes away from you is the right to be angry with him. No matter how badly he treats you, he believes that your voice shouldn't rise and your blood shouldn't boil. The privilege of rage is reserved for him alone. When your anger does jump out of you—as will happen to any abused woman from time to time—he is likely to try to jam it back down your throat as quickly as he can. Then he uses your anger against you to prove what an irrational person you are. Abuse can make you feel strait-jacketed. You may develop physical or emotional reactions to swallowing your anger, such as depression, nightmares, emotional numbing, or eating and sleeping problems, which your partner may use as an excuse to belittle you further or make you feel crazy.[31]

4. **Wear Out the Victim. By staying on the offensive, the gas-lighter eventually wears down the victim, who becomes discouraged, resigned, pessimistic, fearful, debilitated, and self-doubting. The victim begins to question her or his own perception, identity, and reality.**

My ex wanted to buy a wakeboard boat to keep at a lake nearby our home. My son was 4 at the time, and well, we were so busy with work, preschool, and soccer, it didn't seem the right time for a boat. My husband didn't help with my son anyway, and I knew a boat would have him on the lake all weekend, every weekend, and I could predict that he'd be out there even during the week. I told him that I was against the idea. The next day my ex showed me pictures of the boat he wanted, and he demanded that I give him ten minutes to go look at boats. Three hours later we come back home. My mind was still made up: No boat. We didn't need to spend almost six figures on a boat that neither my son nor I wanted. After a month of him telling me it was his money, he was doing this for the "family," and I must not want him to have fun, I threw my hands in the air and told him to "buy the damn boat." He blamed me for wanting to keep our lives boring and dull. Then he bought the boat anyway.

My little boy was scared of the boat; the motor was loud and his dad drove too fast. Shane also expected my son, four years old, to ski. My son preferred to just jump off the back of the boat into the water, again and again. My son's favorite part was being hungry and having a juice box and Cheetos for a snack. My ex was extremely angry about our inability to enjoy the boat like he thought we should enjoy it. He told us that "I bought the boat for you both and you don't appreciate it or my money." He said he might just sell it. So he did. Then he bought a brand new boat for well over six figures. The cycle continued. And with a new boat, my ex was even more meticulous about chips and sodas being spilled on the deck. But again, my ex's anger was all my fault. I didn't monitor my four-year-old to keep him neat and clean. I didn't agree in forcing my son to ski or wakeboard since he would cry and say, "No, mommy." My husband took what could've been a family experience and made it miserable.

5. **Form Codependent Relationships. The** *Oxford Dictionary* **defines codependency as "excessive emotional or psychological reliance on a partner." In a gaslighting relationship, the gaslighter elicits constant insecurity and anxiety in the gaslightee, thereby pulling the gaslightee by the strings. The gaslighter has the power to grant acceptance,**

approval, respect, safety, and security. The gaslighter also has the power (and often threatens) to take them away. A codependent relationship is formed based on fear, vulnerability, and marginalization.

My husband would take several trips a year with six or seven men to cities that hosted motorcycle rallies. In 2004 alone, my ex attended rallies in Sturgis, Daytona, and Austin. If you haven't been to a motorcycle rally, let me tell you how raunchy they can be. Yes, there are highly successful physicians, attorneys, and other professionals who attend and enjoy the experience. And there are also women who ride motorcycles wearing nothing but chaps and body paint. People camp out and party all night. There's excessive drinking, drugs, and sex. I was expected to look the other way and understand that my ex "didn't partake in any of that, Laura. Who do you think I am?"

Meanwhile, no matter how many times I suggested it, I wasn't "allowed" to have a bachelorette party before our wedding or a girls' night out after we were married. Finally, seven years into our marriage, I went out with a good friend for her fortieth birthday. We used a car service for the trip to dinner with four other women, all mothers—all responsible, kind women. When I arrived home that evening around 11:30 p.m., my 5-year-old met me at the front door.

> *Any freedom I thought I had was over. Not only would I pay the price, but my son would, too.*

"Hi Mommy!" he said as he jumped in my arms.

"Hi buddy!" I said. "Did you have fun with daddy? What are you doing up?"

"Daddy is watching TV and I am waiting on YOU!" my son replied. "I'm hungry, mama."

It turns out my ex had not bathed my son or fed him dinner. His dad was watching football highlights in his favorite chair. I asked my ex about our son being hungry, dirty, and tired. My husband didn't reply. Nevertheless, I got the message. It was forbidden for me to go out with anyone, even women for a birthday dinner. Any freedom I thought I had was over. Not only would I pay the price, but my son would, too.

Over the subsequent years the number of my friends and even acquaintances dwindled to a handful. It wasn't worth the punishment and castigation if I tried to meet a friend for coffee or lunch. At sales meetings, my ex expected me to be in my room after mandatory dinners with colleagues. He even appeared at a dinner program I was hosting in downtown Dallas for physicians to make sure no one was being inappropriate: me or my customers. My world had turned into a prison with my ex as the warden.

Narcissists use gaslighting to isolate their victims. If a narcissist can keep you from your friends and family and any other support system, he has a better chance of you staying as his narcissistic supply. This behavior is controlling, toxic, demeaning, and can cause the greatest damage to you emotionally. You lose touch with reality and live in an ever-shrinking, soulless environment.

6. **Give False Hope. As a manipulative tactic, the gas lighter will occasionally treat the victim with mildness, moderation, and even superficial kindness or remorse, to give the gaslightee false hope. In these circumstances, the victim might think: "Maybe he's really not THAT bad," "Maybe things are going to get better," or "Let's give it a chance."**

Toward the end of our marriage I had gathered enough strength to look for my own home, meet with an attorney, and attend counseling on my own. My ex was controlling enough to know my every move, and I didn't care. I just wanted to explore my options for the future and make an informed decision. My ex was predictable each time he learned where I was going. He would beg for forgiveness. He often fell to his knees, crying and pleading for me to stay. "This time it's different," my ex often said. "I want to change. But I can't work on me and our marriage if we are living apart." He would be nice, sweet, patient, and kind until I once again let my guard down. Then the abuse would start again.

I got more flowers during those five years than I've received in my lifetime. Some of them I hope brought joy to a local nursing home, because that's where I took them. I felt like they were tainted, insincere tokens of apologies for abuse that would continually reappear. I would tell my husband, "I don't need or want flowers. I just need you to be nice to me." The kindness would last for about three days, and then he would revert to a toxic, calculating, psychological abuser.

7. **Dominate and Control. At its extreme, the ultimate objective of a pathological gaslighter is to control, dominate, and take advantage of another individual, or a group, or even an entire society. By maintaining and intensifying an incessant stream of lies and coercions, the gaslighter keeps the gaslightees in a constant state of insecurity, doubt, and fear. The gaslighter can then exploit their victims at will, for the augmentation of their power and personal gain.**

Narcissists' language and actions are almost always geared toward that ultimate goal: to dominate. They must maintain full control and power over a person, community, or group, and quite often, over money. For these individuals, money is often associated with power and status.

Through an online Facebook support group I started, I've heard many stories of a narcissist related to money. I'll use my example since I know it the most intimately.

When it came to money, my ex was obsessed. Anyone's worth was first judged by how much money he had. My ex was also very skilled at taking advantage of the money I earned. For example, my ex would tell me the property taxes on our home were thousands of dollars more than they were. That way, I wouldn't argue and would pay for whatever he asked me to buy, whether it was expensive vacations, plane tickets to see my family, or my own birthday cake. He would also tell me I needed to pay for a dinner out or our son's clothes.

"Remember Laura I just paid thousands and thousands of dollars so you can live in this house." I learned after my divorce that I ended up paying more than I would have, had we split the property tax bill and all other bills. He told me the property taxes on the house were fifty percent more than they were. And I believed him.

Why did we treat money this way in a marriage? When we first got married, my ex demanded we keep separate accounts. He would tell me what to pay for and when to pay it. He told me I was terrible with money (I wasn't), and he didn't want any part of that. Already emotionally broken, I did what he said and risked being financially broken, too, to make him happy.

Interestingly, when I received a significant pay raise with my second job in biotechnology, he was all about combining our income. I was beginning to become stronger and said "No." My nonconformity didn't go over well. He said I was impeding his healing to be a better husband. I can laugh at it now. The only thing I was hindering was his ability to spend my money on more of his toys.

Projection

Projection is a psychological term used when people deny their own problems, issues, or feelings and attribute them to someone else. A narcissist wants to be the king and ruler of his domain. Anything that disrupts his dominion makes him angry, and he certainly cannot turn the anger on himself. Instead he turns it on you.

The narcissist is good at saying, "You're sulking, you're mad, and you're ruining my day." When in fact, he is the reason the home atmosphere is toxic and everyone is on tiptoe around him. But will HE take responsibility for that? No. The world is supposed to cater to HIM. YOU are responsible for his happiness.

I remember a few times when Shane would be home working all day, and I would come in from a day in the field calling on physicians. I might be tired or frustrated, or even happy and chatty, and he would say something like, "Why are you always so worried about work? Your work isn't as important as mine. Why do you put work first? I've learned to put family first. I'm not sure why you treat work like the be all and end all."

The bottom line in my situation was two-fold: First, I worked harder than Shane and won more sales awards, at least after we were married. Everything was a competition and he couldn't stand to see me "win." Second, Shane wanted me to acknowledge how successful and brilliant he was, which I did only in the beginning. When I saw how little he worked and truly cared about his job, I stopped the compliments. That didn't go over well.

Also, defending yourself won't go over well, either. It's best to try to leave the conversation and detach yourself from his mood until things calm down. Understand what he's doing and walk away if you can.

Word Salad

Narcissists thrive on conflict and attention. If you ever disagree with a narcissist or want something different, expect a word salad. These "salads" are conversations that go in circles. The narcissist will use projection, deflection, arguments, and gaslighting to send your focus anywhere but the issue at hand.

The narcissist is skilled at trying to make you feel guilty for having your own thoughts and feelings. For example, she may just tell you she's sharing what other people think and see about you. Or, she'll say, "I was thinking about something you said the other day and I didn't bring it up. Why are you bringing this up? You are wasting my time." She is trying to frustrate you and draw your attention away from the discussion which is usually centered on something the narcissist needs to change or at least address.

In the eyes of a narcissist, *you* are the problem if you happen to exist and disagree in any way. It's her world, and you are only a visitor in it. She doesn't want to you be an unruly guest.

During almost any argument my ex and I had, he was skilled at making a word salad. Even recently, we needed to discuss something about my child. Over email, my ex started changing the subject away from the issue at hand. My son plays select basketball, and there's a returning player to the team that may take his starting spot if my son doesn't progress. I encouraged my ex to talk to the coach while I was working, and my ex's response was that "he attended each practice." Unfortunately, that's not the issue. I had to remind him twice about the question I asked. This wasn't about my ex. This was about our son and any extra practice needed.

The best thing to do is walk away. Draw a boundary. Tell the narcissist, "I can't talk about this right now." Disengage.

Nitpicking and Game Changing

Nitpicking and game changing can come in many different forms, but it's most likely present in a relationship with a narcissist. Perhaps you wear clothes the narcissist likes, you cook foods he prefers, and you try to be consistently in a good mood for them. WAIT! Don't get too comfortable. Now that's changing!

The narcissist will change the game and the rules. He may suggest little tweaks to improve your cooking or dress. He may constantly criticize what you used to bring you praise.

The narcissist wants to pull you away from your strengths and have you focus on your shortcomings. That's so he can keep you right where he wants you to be. He wants to serving his every need and never leaving him.

Be careful and avoid listening to what the narcissist says. This kind of nitpicking can make you feel crazy. When you've been able to hit the bull's-eye on the target repeatedly, and then you consistently miss, remember it's not your aim. Someone has moved the target. You are fine just the way you are. Don't let him win with this crazy-making.

Triangulating

Have you ever had a narcissist tell you that someone thinks a certain way about you? That's triangulation. Triangulation is bringing the opinion, thoughts, perspective, or threats of another person into the relationship. Many narcissists like to triangulate their significant other with ex-partners, family members, and friends.

The narcissist may say, "Everyone knows what you really are" or "You aren't as well thought of as you might think."

The narcissist wants you to go on the offensive, so he can play the victim. And, it makes you feel crazy since he is learning you just might be on to him. This tactic is meant to pull you away from the truth: the other person in this relationship is abusive.

My ex was an expert at triangulation with former girlfriends and wives. He told me that his second wife was better in bed and in the kitchen than I was, his girlfriend just before me had better boobs and a better body, and his first wife was the sweetest and kindest woman he had known.

He would also tell me that my father, my rock in this world, thinks I am mentally unstable. I would leave those conversations feeling like I was insufficient in our love life and home life. I felt unworthy as a wife, mom, and daughter.

The same efforts by you to exit such conversations are important for your sanity. Do not listen to a word of this. You know who your friends and family are, and you know the people who love and respect you. Walk away from the narcissist. Disengage. Remember *your* truth.

Bait and Sugarcoating

Many narcissists are proficient at bait and sugarcoating. This is when a narcissist knows how to irritate you, so you eventually react. The narcissist will say something several times until he provokes you. Then, he will innocently stand back and exclaim that he "cannot understand why you are so upset when he asked a simple question or made a simple observation."

My ex was excellent at bait and sugarcoat. He would often subtly "point out" that I was doing something wrong in his eyes as a mother. And he would remind me two or three times. Once I finally blew up and said, "Just leave it alone!" he would calmly look at me and ask, "What's the problem, Laura? Can you not have a civilized conversation? Maybe you are the one who truly needs counseling. Not us as a couple."

This was crazy-making. And this is the narcissist's intent.

Remember the bait-and-sugarcoat technique. If you can walk away, walk away. This is a form of mind control that can really distort your reality. Listen carefully and ask yourself the first time he says something, and only the first time, is he being truthful? The answer is most likely no. Get some space. Trust your gut. Deep down, you still know the truth.

Physical Abuse—When the Verbal Abuse Turns Physical

Has he ever trapped you in a room and not let you out?
Has he ever raised a fist as if he were going to hit you?

Has he ever thrown an object that hit you or nearly did?
Has he ever held you down or grabbed you to restrain you?
Has he ever shoved, poked, or grabbed you?
Has he ever threatened to hurt you?
If the answer to any of these questions is yes, then we can
stop wondering whether he'll ever be violent;
he already has been.

> – Lundy Bancroft, *Why Does He Do That?*
> *Inside the Minds of Angry and Controlling Men*

The Centers for Disease Control (CDC) reported in 2017 that one in four women and one in seven men will experience violence by an intimate partner in their lifetime.[32] When I answered the questions above, I said yes to a few of them.

Trust your gut. Deep down, you still know the truth.

My ex did not hit me, but I can recall one incident where he grabbed my arm so tightly it left a mark. We were standing at his company holiday party in the ballroom of a swanky downtown Dallas hotel. My ex asked me to attend the party with him and spend the night. The next day he would go to his meeting downstairs and I would head home and go to work. We got dressed at the hotel, and I remember feeling pretty in some new white pants and a frilly black top. After a few drinks that night, I recall standing in a group of about four people, laughing loudly at a joke his colleague from Florida had shared. I was happy and a bit tipsy, and not yet a mother, so my only responsibility was getting to work the next morning.

Suddenly, my ex reached out and grabbed my arm. "Why are you flirting with Chris? I knew you had a crush on him."

"Shane, you are being paranoid," I said. "There's no way. I am here for you and proud to be your wife."

He wouldn't let go, and I was afraid I would bruise or at least have a big red mark on my arm.

"Shane, you are hurting my arm, so please let go!" I said.

Shane's boss walked up at that moment, so he let me go. I quickly excused myself for the ladies' room. Instead, I went out the side door of the bar, grabbed my things from our hotel room, and went outside to get a taxi home, which was thirty miles from the hotel.

I didn't sleep much that night, and I don't remember hearing anything from my ex until early the next morning, when he called to say that I had embarrassed him by leaving.

Of course, my intuition told me he was angry because the night wasn't going to end well if I stayed. But I didn't know how to explain to my parents or family that barely a year into our marriage, the man I was head over heels with was hurting me emotionally and for the first time, physically.

My ex also had times where he would block my way after we had fought about something. As with a narcissist, you'll never win the argument, so the best thing to do is not argue. I cannot count how many times our discussions would escalate, and I would want to evacuate. I often tried to walk out the back door into the garage. My ex is 6'2 and weighed around 205 at the time. He was nearly double my size, so it would stop me in my tracks when I just wanted to give him time to cool off. Looking back, I see that my attempt at a departure showed strength, and my ex didn't want that. He wanted to keep me involved in the discussion, when the only one who was talking was him.

If you think your partner or ex-partner has the propensity to be violent, put a plan in place. If he has already been violent, talk to a friend or family member and get out. There is a list of organizations at the back of this book that help women and their children break free from abusive relationships. Without serious intervention, the violence won't stop.

CHAPTER 9

Children of Narcissists

When I was with my mother, I sometimes thought of myself as a trophy—something to be flaunted before friends. When out of public view, I sat on the shelf ignored and forgotten.

> – Joan Frances Casey, *The Flock: The*
> *Autobiography of a Multiple Personality*

Somehow I believed it was my obligation to try to do the right thing by her because she had given birth to me.

> – D.G. Kaye, *Conflicted Hearts*

We all want the approval of mom. We think, "If my mother can't love me, who can? I mean, she gave birth to me." I lived this through my early years and into college. I remember asking my counselor why my brother wasn't as damaged as I was. He said it was most likely that I was seen as a direct reflection and extension of her.

Although I'll address mothers in this section, many of these traits apply to narcissistic fathers, too. A woman who recently joined my Facebook support group, we'll call her Mandy, told me she spent eighteen years under the rule of a narcissistic father. Mandy said her father would hug her as a young girl and pinch her back because he wanted to see how much "back fat" she had or how much weight she had gained. She's forty-five and still cannot receive a hug without being uncomfortable.

We all want the approval of mom. We think, "If my mother can't love me, who can?

Dr. Carter says narcissism can also rub off on children of the narcissists. Often these parents want their child to be a "mini-me." The parent wants to live out unrealized expectations through the child, whether it's in sports, school, relationships, or beauty.

Sometimes as children of narcissistic parents, we can go the opposite direction. We can turn into the needy wife or friend, with a lack of self-confidence or sense of self. Often, the children of narcissistic parents can't give anything because their soul was never filled. These children can turn to eating disorders, alcoholism, and other addictive behaviors growing up. We will explore that later.

Dr. Karyl McBride has studied parental narcissism, specifically that of mothers, for several decades. She writes in her book *Will I Ever Be Good Enough?* about narcissistic mothers:

> Even if your mother does not have all nine traits of a fully
> blown narcissistic personality disorder, her narcissism has

no doubt hurt you. I realized that there are mothers that are so emotionally needy and self-absorbed they are unable to give unconditional love and emotional support to their daughters.[33]

A child of a narcissist typically deals with these ten issues, according to Dr. McBride. I can attest that they apply to me.

1. **You find yourself constantly attempting to win your mother's love, attention, and approval, but never being able to please her.**

I felt like for my mother, I could never be pretty enough, thin enough, smart enough, or selfless enough. I often heard her degrade other women, putting them down by saying things like "her hair is too long" or "she looks like she's flat ready to ride" (slutty), or "she is selfish," and the list goes on. I saw how my mom treated those women with disdain and dismissal. I was terrified to fall short of her standards for appearance and behavior. But the thing was, even when I followed her rules, it wasn't good enough. My hair could be shorter (to this day), I could've made a 100 on my math quiz instead if a 97, and more.

2. **Your mother emphasizes the importance of how it looks to her, rather than how it feels to you.**

When I came home from college after finals one year, I was exhausted. I had pulled out a 3.4, taking some of the hardest courses at Southern Methodist University in Dallas. I wore the typical college uniform, Umbro shorts and a tee short, almost the entire holiday break (Don't judge here. Umbro shorts were the *coolest* and the most comfortable thing you could ever wear in the 90s.) Mother was mortified. She asked me to change. I said I was exhausted, but that fell on deaf ears. She was concerned someone might stop by and I looked like a slug. I wanted to wrap myself in nurture and comfort, not standards.

I can tell you, if my son decides to come home for Christmas break, I will celebrate his arrival no matter how he is dressed. Or how he smells. (We are twelve now, and I kid you not—I roll down the windows in the car and put his shoes outside every evening. This is my ritual. Every. Single. Night. And when when I do basketball carpool? Febreze can't touch the smell.) My son is accepted and loved unconditionally. He is welcome in any emotional or physical state. Always.

My son struggles with ADHD, so the school year is tough. Sometimes, I tell my sweet boy, we just have crappy days. There's no other way to put it. He cries. I cry. We get it out. Then we pray and we move on. I want him to grow up owning his feelings, feeling his feelings, and moving on.

3. Your mother is jealous of you.

I can't recall if my mother is or was jealous of me. For me, it was more that I was a direct reflection of her. I looked good, she looked good. When I won an award or a competition, she felt like a winner.

As a child, even from the age of three, I wanted long hair. My mother wouldn't let me. She said, "I needed to show off my pretty face" and women with short hair were "stronger and better because they were different." Looking back, after my finishing my research for this book, I understand why she didn't allow me to have long hair. Hers was short, in a boy cut, and therefore mine was, too. I often wonder if it was a threat to her for me to have long, blonde hair and be feminine with such a look. Prettier maybe? Maybe I drew more attention? I don't' know. These parents can also be jealous of their child or children.

Thank goodness I had two grandmothers who would greet me, no matter how I looked or felt, with "Hello, Beautiful." One grandmother and I shared a deep love of reading, and we bonded over the hundreds of books that lined her shelves. The other grandmother thought everything I did was hilarious and sweet. My interactions with both grandmothers helped me keep a modicum of my own identity.

4. Your mother does not support your healthy expressions of self, especially when they conflict with her own needs or threaten her

I recall when I was about seven or eight, my mother told me I was "the most selfish little girl in the world." It's taken years of therapy for me to recover from that statement alone. I suppose I was standing up for my feelings or beliefs, but that wasn't allowed in a narcissist's kingdom. After learning my mom thought I was the most selfish kid alive, I quit standing up for myself. To this day I have heard my mom talk about other people being selfish and self-centered. I think she says that because the "selfish person" doesn't meet her standards or elevate her to the superior position she believes she should occupy. Any time you try to use self-love, you will be labeled "bad," but doing what the narcissist wants you to do will be categorized as "good."

5. In your family, it's always about mom.

Narcissistic mothers are so self-absorbed they don't recognize how their own behavior affects their children. And sometimes their spouse.

Our home life seemed to orbit around mom. She dictated, even as teenagers, how we dressed, cut our hair, spoke, and felt about certain situations. If we didn't agree with her opinion on something, we were shunned,

Several years ago, my mother decided to get her masters and then her PhD in Early Childhood Education. She is a fantastic teacher. For some reason, mother withholds judgment on her students and even cherishes them. But to earn her advanced degrees, mom had to live two hour away from my hometown and without my father for almost ten years. I remember one of the first nights when my brother and I had departed for fall semester at our respective colleges, and my father was at home with only the cocker spaniel named Alison to keep him company; my father called me. He joked, "I'm moving to Dallas and will live in your apartment while you graduate from SMU."

For entertainment he would sometimes iron clothes and turn up the music and call me. Dad lives in a small town, so there's not much to do there on almost any night of the week. I'm sure he felt pressure to be home and not having fun. Mom made it clear to all of us that she was working hard as the integral part of any school for which she was an administrator.

6. Your mother is unable to empathize.

Your feelings are invalidated when you grow up with a narcissistic mother. You feel like your feelings and beliefs don't matter to anyone if they aren't even on your mother's radar screen.

Growing up, I had many questions about sex, but since my mom had taught me only bad girls have sex, I had to ask my father. She didn't want to hear questions or concerns. He handed me a book and talked to me about intimacy. In my mind though, all through college, I avoided men and was nervous that I was just being used, due to my mom's beliefs. I am sure I carried an uptight stigma around campus. And well, I was uptight. I felt like even at college, mother would know if I got involved in a "bad" way with a man.

7. Your mother can't deal with her own feelings.

You learn to put on an act so your mom won't have to see how you really feel or have to deal with a situation. Mom used to often say "put on a happy face. If you look good, you will feel good and the world will see." This allows only a superficial relationship with no emotional connection.

Also, as a teenager, I was often labeled by my mother as the "sensitive one." This term was said with derision, as if being sensitive was a bad trait. Looking back, I don't think I was any more sensitive than any other teenage girl. At my brother's wedding reception, my father stood up and toasted my brother as the "easy one" and his sister as the "high-maintenance" one. At the time I was dating the man who would turn out to be my husband. That gave him another point to overemphasize during our entire marriage.

Many times the narcissist's victims are categorized as too sensitive, when really we are just expressing feelings like a normal person. Don't be ashamed of having thoughts, feelings, opinions, and most of all, empathy.

Dr. Koy Roberts is a counselor in Coppell, Texas. He says empathy is one of the few traits that cannot be taught. You are either born with it or without it. Guess which bucket the narcissist fits in?

Be confident in your feelings, opinions, mindsets, and beliefs. Own them. You were told for so long what to believe and think. It's your truth now.

8.   Your mother is critical and judgmental.

Narcissistic parents are critical and judgmental about everything. Dr. McBride says it stems from a fragile sense of self. The trouble is, we believe and absorb this criticism because it comes from our *mother*. She is supposed to love us unconditionally.

It took years of counseling to realize that mother won't ever love me unconditionally. She wasn't given that love so she doesn't know how to give it. I've accepted that and forgiven her. Only in the last few years have I learned to handle it in a healthy way.

To this day, mother is still somewhat critical and judgmental. I see and hear her criticize mostly women, mostly family members, especially my nieces who are AMAZING girls. AMAZING. I have a son, but these girls—WOW. They are smart, beautiful, sweet, and love each other.

Mother criticizes how they dress (we like flip-flops in Texas and Arkansas in the summer because it's so blazing hot) and how we talk (we use "ya'll" a lot). She even criticizes how clean their home is because my sister-in-law prefers it that way.

My brother has four kids. My house is a disaster zone about three days a week with a twelve-year-old boy and two labradoodles. Meanwhile, they have FOUR kids and a dog, and their home is a showpiece.

Mom did target a very dear friend of mine while we were on vacation. Out of the blue, she criticized my friend Amy for allowing her five-year-old to sleep in her bed in the beach house. Amy and I divorced around the same time and have been a support system for each other for three years. Amy told me after it happened and kindly blew it off. I was livid. I am used to mother's opinions and educational research. She can basically tell me that what I do as a parent isn't good enough. But when she turns the criticism and judgment on my friends, I get upset.

That's one reason, just recently, that I had to speak with my father to say that my parents weren't welcome to stay four days when they came to visit. I have to take my mom in small doses.

9. Your mother treats you like a friend and not a daughter.

In a healthy mother–daughter relationship, the mother takes care of the daughter's emotional and physical needs. But because the mother didn't receive proper parenting herself, the mothers are usually needy children inside.

As a result, you will find yourself as the one giving love, admiration, emotional support, and attention. You must prop your parent up when it should be the other way around.

10. **You have no boundaries or privacy from your mother.**

We should all separate emotionally from our parents as we grow up, but with a narcissistic parent, we aren't allowed to become our own people. I saw this even early on when I was a teenager.

I learned about periods from my fifth-grade teacher. When I started my period, I cried. I was so scared and needed someone to hug me and remind me it was an important part of growing up. I finally approached mother so I could have the necessary supplies to get through my first cycle. I was twelve. I felt dirty and ashamed. I needed nurturing and support. That was never in mom's repertoire.

Years later, I grew my hair out. It is still long. She approached me just a few years ago with a picture of when my hair was short and said, "You look better this way."

As I got older, the teen years didn't get any easier. My mother believes sex should be saved for marriage and marriage only, as many church doctrines translate the Bible into those beliefs. My mother started talking to me about boys and how they always wanted one thing and would just use me for it. I grew up thinking that no one would love me for my mind. They would just use me. The only safe place was home.

I remember coming home from summer camp after two weeks away. The morning of dismissal, I washed my hair three times. I wanted it to be clean and to smell good for her. I ran up to her after missing her intensely, and I said, "Mom, I washed my hair three times for you! " Her response was, "I can't tell."

One memory from my college years comes to mind that rocked my world at the time. I was undergoing treatment for the eating disorder and gaining weight. My periods were still non-existent, and my physician was worried I might hurt my fertility if I didn't have a cycle. So, she put me on birth control. During this visit home, my mother found the pills. She came unglued. She didn't believe me that I wasn't having sex. I felt like I couldn't win, so matter what I did.

It broke my heart. I felt her love for me was always just out of reach. I just couldn't get there, and I'll never be able to get there. And I've learned that's okay. I am okay. I am a great mom, daughter, girlfriend, friend and person.

CHAPTER 10

Can Narcissism Rub Off on Children?

The narcissistic parent will attempt to perpetuate this dependence to the point where the child is not permitted to develop his or her own identity but is rather forced to become "one with" the narcissist until there is no perceived difference (on the part of the narcissistic parent) between the parent and the child.

– www.postive-parenting-ally.com

Abused children pick up from their past encounters to expect less of themselves and others. They are not commonly taught to trust and end up finding out themselves as tough, unbalanced, and unworthy of love or care.

– Patricia Dsouza, *When Roses Are Crushed*

As we've learned so far, the narcissist has a deep, deep need for control. So why would her children be immune to this control?

During my many conversations with Dr. Les Carter, who specializes in narcissism and its effects on others, he said yes, narcissistic characteristics can be absorbed or mimicked by the child. The child sees mom or dad treat others a certain way, and the child models his behavior after mom or dad. Perhaps the child learns to deny, lie, and blame others because that's what a parent does. The child thinks that is the way the world operates.

Dr. Carter said, "Narcissists want children to be a 'mini-me.' They want a miniature version of themselves. And sometimes they succeed."

Sometimes, Dr. Carter said, it can be when the parent tells the child, "See, you if do this you can be special like me." Other times it can be intimidation or criticism to steer the child toward what the narcissist wants the child to do. It stems from the narcissist's deep need for power.

Think about what you learned from your parents. We can carry those life lessons throughout our adulthood, even if we don't agree with those teachings. For example, I learned from my father to let mother's happiness come first, at the cost of my health and my emotional well-being. A son may later model his behavior after his father and choose a life partner who is the dominant person in the relationship.

When my son visits his father across town, I feel like I often must do some deprogramming when he returns. My son can be disrespectful to me and blame any problem on me, not his bad choices. I saw this recently when I asked him to stay away from a friend he met in middle school. My son makes bad choices when he hangs out with this student, almost every single time. I know this is an age-old parenting problem, but I felt like my son's response wasn't typical when we discussed him breaking my rule. My son told me it was *my* job to keep him away from this friend, even though at school, where I am not allowed, is where he is hanging out with this preteen and getting in trouble. My ex used to frequently blame me for any problem he found himself involved with, as most narcissists do. I am diligently watching my son and his reactions when it comes to deflecting the blame to someone else. I am determined to raise a kind, loving, smart, empathetic kid.

I have my son in routine counseling, and now that he is almost a teenager, I don't tell him his dad is a narcissist, but we do discuss ways to deflect the criticism. For example, my son is a skilled point guard for a select basketball team. When he doesn't play well, my ex will compare him to other boys on the team who had a good game or made a memorable shot. I have watched my son's face fall as he hears these critical words come out of my ex's mouth, and I have told my son recently to just listen, but don't really hear. If you have to, say "la la la" to yourself, because your dad doesn't mean it. Sometimes he is just venting when the team loses. I tell him your dad loves you so very much, as much as he can, and to let the critical comments roll off your back. I reminded him to shake it off, like our labradoodle does after I give him a bath. My son thought that analogy was funny, but I've seen our conversation make it easier for him to take what his father says in stride.

I believe each child is special, and a bad game or grade doesn't make my son a bad kid. As parents, I believe, we must nurture these children and love them as much as we can. We must offset what the narcissistic parent does. Through counseling and our reactions to situations the narcissist orchestrates, we must protect these children. It's not possible to keep these parents away from their children, but armed with knowledge and intuition, we can do it. It's up to us.

CHAPTER 11

Coping Mechanisms

Every form of addiction is bad, no matter whether the narcotic be alcohol, morphine or idealism.

– C.G. Jung

No one told me you can love someone and still be miserable. How is that possible?

– Krista Ritchie, *Addicted to You*

After living with a narcissist or being abused by one, many victims turn to addiction of some form to cope. Dr. McBride theorizes that victims of narcissists usually do one of two things:

1. We over-achieve to prove ourselves the total opposite.

2. We self-sabotage.[34]

I think we can do both. I went from an eating disorder to an overachiever.

Eating Disorders

There must be come correlation between children of narcissists and weight. Several members of my Facebook group who have grown up under a narcissistic parent recall the subtle or blatant focus on being thin.

Being "skinny" was very important in my childhood home. As early as I can remember, mother would sing this nursery rhyme she made up to the tune of Jack and Jill: "Fatty, fatty two-by-four, couldn't get through the open door." She would sing that each time my father, brother, or I had dessert or grabbed a second cookie. It was a shaming tactic, in which I certainly felt an enormous amount of guilt for having something that tastes good but might contribute to being fat.

> *It turns out the fat comments would come to manifest themselves in an eating disorder.*

Mom would then remind us about her time in high school when she was overweight, and no one liked her because of it. She told me stories about how she was a chubby teenager and the boys at her high school made fun of her. They would yell, "Hiiiipppoooo," from the top of the stairs.

At the time I was about ten pounds overweight. I had filled out, but I hadn't finished puberty and my growth. I felt like I needed to look thin and be pretty all the time or she wouldn't love me, and neither would anyone else. The message was loud and clear: if you are fat, no one will ever love you.

It turns out the fat comments would come to manifest themselves in an eating disorder. My mom watched every move I made, critiqued my appearance, evaluated my grades, and censured my friends who didn't measure up to her standards. Her love was still so far out of reach. I couldn't control anything in my life, even my feelings, no matter how hard I tried. That's why I started to control food. I yearned for this feeling of control to numb the pain I couldn't identify. The bonus was I would also be skinny. I could numb my feelings and win my mother's elusive love, or so I thought.

By the time I hit freshman year of college, I weighed 89 pounds. I was near death. My father saw me that Christmas break and immediately made phone calls to get me into a program for eating disorders.

I remember sitting at Baylor Dallas in a cramped room with a counselor and intake specialist. The room was probably eighty-two degrees and it was winter, so mom, dad, and I had sweaters on and long pants. I was finally warm. Everyone else was perspiring. I had such a low level of body fat that I had quit having periods and was freezing all the time. My fingers were blue.

This part of my journey is how I met the counselor who would later help me understand and identify my narcissistic parenting and later, my narcissistic husband. We visited Dr. Ray Levy later that day, near a big hospital called Medical City Dallas. Ray was thirty at the time, newly married and right out of Harvard with a PhD in psychology. I told him recently I think he looks like a handsome version of Matt Lauer, with certainly more integrity and wit. He tells me now about his memories of the first time he saw me. He says when I walked I looked like a skeletal clone of my mother, right down to the short hair. He says he knew then what my problem was.

My father explained to Ray that day what my last few years had looked like, with dieting, exercise, and food restriction. My mother sat there and didn't say a word. Ray says he asked her a few questions and she pushed back immediately. He knew then he was dealing with narcissist who only thought of herself and took no responsibility for her daughter, who was near death, sitting beside her. I was so fearful that day that I don't remember this—but Ray recalls that my mother got up and LEFT. And she never returned to see Dr. Levy, even though I saw him for the next two years.

My father, on the other hand, wrote Dr. Levy a thank-you note years later for saving my life.

Did my father ever see the problem? I think he may have partially seen it. But he had developed healthy coping mechanisms for our family life, like hunting and fishing and letting mom's rules stand. It would be disloyal, and he does have to live with her. They truly love each other, and their marriage works for them. There is even a family joke today that mother's rules are the "do right rules." I don't find the phrase funny because of what I went through, although most of my family chuckles at that joke.

Dad will say things like "It was your perception," "How you understood things to be," and "She only wanted the best for you." I don't doubt she did want the best for me. But most of all, she wanted the best for her. And I couldn't give it.

Even into my adulthood, I still longed for my mother's approval. I would buy her nice Christmas gifts when I held my own job (they weren't good enough). A sweater would be too big or not the right color or something like that. When my son was born, mom and dad were late to the delivery because it was an emergency Caesarean. When I was back in my room after the surgery, I called my parents who were driving into Dallas for the birth. That was a hard phone call. Mom wanted to be there and she didn't like the fact that it happened without her. Dad was, however, grateful that my son and I were okay. Looking back, I cannot believe I had trepidation about one of the scariest, and happiest, times of my life because my mother wouldn't approve. And she didn't.

Addiction to Pills and Alcohol

I have friends who have grown up with narcissists or been married to one. These friends have struggled with addiction to pills and alcohol as they try to avoid the pain that accompanies loving a narcissist.

I don't have first-hand experience in dealing with addiction to a substance, but I have interviewed psychologists who have decades of experience in treating addiction.

Many people who are hurting turn to pills to numb the pain. When prescribed for physical pain, drugs that contain opioids can alleviate post-surgical or chronic pain. These drugs are generally safe when you take them for a short time, as prescribed by a physician. But in addition to helping you manage the pain, they can also give you a feeling of well-being or euphoria. That's where addiction comes in. When you are living in pain from a bad relationship or situation, a pill may seem an easy solution. But the long-term side effects of taking pills aren't worth it. I've seen women lose custody of their children. I've seen others hospitalized for psychiatric problems and subsequent treatment.

My friend, I'll call her Jenny, has struggled with addiction since she was a teenager. Jenny tells me that she relapses when she becomes too confident that she can handle pills on her own. When life is going well, she says, she tells herself, "Oh, I can take just one Xanax or hydrocodone and stop." Jenny knows now that's not possible. One turns into twenty.

I have another acquaintance who has been sober almost a year. He tells me that he drank alcohol to numb the pain of a disintegrating marriage. His ex-wife certainly has narcissistic tendencies that I've seen from my few interactions with her. I can see where alcohol abuse would be an outlet for so many hurting from narcissistic abuse. He tells me that he would think he could handle just a few drinks to take the edge off the pain. His favorite phrase is, "You think you can handle it (alcohol) until you can't anymore." He began putting himself and his children in danger. So, he stopped. He joined Alcoholics Anonymous and is doing well, attending AA meetings almost daily.

Psychologists and physicians alike recommend finding a treatment program if you believe you have a problem or know someone who does. I've seen these programs put my two friends back together who have struggled for years with addiction. You can't do it alone. No one expects you to.

Other Coping Mechanisms

Being married to or involved with a narcissist shapes who you are. You begin to explore many different ways of coping with the hell you live in daily. One of my most regrettable mistakes came during the middle of my marriage: I had an affair.

It was 2010 and my son was about three. The abuse was at its cruelest point, and I began an affair with a man I met at the gym. It didn't start that way, much like affairs do. He was a friend and someone to talk to who believed the hell I was living. Then it became more than emotional. I am not proud of that behavior, and I beg you not to do it no matter how lonely or emotionally starved you become. Get out first. I didn't. My irrational thinking to ease the pain was this: Have an affair and get the love you need outside the marriage. Then, I thought, I could survive this toxic hell for the next decade until my son graduated high school. I thought that having someone on the outside to support me and encourage me would help me get through the daily pain and suffering. It definitely took the edge off. I had never been told that I matter. That I was a great mom. That I was important. That I was truly loved.

Easter Sunday, six months after I had met the man I was having an affair with, I prayed to God to give me the strength to end it. I missed that man's emotional support and strength, but I knew if I wanted to get out of this toxic marriage I had to do the rest of this marriage God's way. Looking back, I have no regrets about ending that affair. I gave my marriage all I had the last five years, with no return of course because the abuse grew worse. But I know, and God knows I gave it my best.

My ex did find out about my affair. He called me a "cunt," "whore," and "white trash." He threatened to tell my parents and the entire population of our suburb about my affair. I told him to go ahead. My husband never did. Narcissists, as you know, care deeply about what other people think about them. So, in his mind, me having an affair showed that my ex wasn't able to keep his wife happy enough to stay loyal and monogamous.

Here's the part of the story that baffles yet finally amuses me. All during our marriage, my ex was sleeping around. A man a trust with my life told me that my ex often bragged about prostitutes and various women he had slept with. I have flashbacks of some of the last fights we had…or rather thrashings I received. My ex would tell me to sit in the chair while he paced and screamed at me, saying things like "How dare I leave the marriage bed?" I would cry and feel like the biggest loser. All the while, he was the biggest liar.

Depression and Anxiety

Understandingly, many victims of narcissists become depressed, despondent, and unable to focus on normal daily activities. Depression and anxiety take over. I personally had days where I couldn't get out of bed or had at least one panic attack a day.

Depression affects fifteen million Americans.[35] Everyone experiences the occasional blue mood or bad day, but true depression is significant, constant, and detrimental. As empaths and victims of such demoralizing behavior, we are susceptible to turning inward and developing depression.

The Anxiety and Depression Association of America describes these symptoms as significant markers of a major depressive episode:

- Persistent sad, anxious, or "empty" mood.
- Feelings of hopelessness, pessimism.

- Feelings of guilt, worthlessness, helplessness.

- Loss of interest or pleasure in hobbies and activities, including sex.

- Decreased energy, fatigue, feeling "slowed down."

- Difficulty concentrating, remembering, making decisions.

- Insomnia, early-morning awakening, or oversleeping.

- Low appetite and weight loss, or overeating and weight gain.

- Thoughts of death or suicide, suicide attempts.

- Restlessness, irritability.

- Persistent physical symptoms that do not respond to treatment, such as headaches, digestive disorders, and pain for which no other cause can be diagnosed.[36]

Dr. Craig N. Sawchuk, PhD, LP, with the Mayo Clinic, says anxiety may occur as a symptom of clinical (major) depression. It's also common to have depression that's triggered by an anxiety disorder, such as generalized anxiety disorder, panic disorder, or separation anxiety disorder. Many people have a diagnosis of both an anxiety disorder and clinical depression.

I remember first becoming aware of my depression when I was a teenager. I had noticed my life wasn't like anyone else's. I felt like I couldn't share my doubts, fears, and feelings with my mom. My home didn't feel emotionally safe. It was easier and better to just pretend be happy.

Then, when I was married, my anxiety tripled. Anxiety and depression go hand in hand. My home felt like an emotional minefield. I was depressed. Nowhere and no conversation were safe. I wanted to share worries and doubts with my husband, but I quickly learned I couldn't. Telling him my deepest thoughts and fears meant that he had ammunition. He would use them against me.

My actual treatment for depression started in my early twenties. My first television job was in Myrtle Beach, South Carolina. I moved across the country at age twenty-two to start my own career in broadcast news. I was fearful yet excited to begin to report and possibly anchor the news in the 131st market in the United States. Nielson ranks markets by population and the number of homes with televisions. Usually the top 200 markets are on the radar screen of new journalists trying to land a job. Market 131 was a big and exciting step for me.

My home felt like an emotional minefield.

However, I didn't know a soul when I arrived in Myrtle Beach. My dad helped me get settled, and then left to go back and run his clothing business in Arkansas. Several months on the job passed, and I was not yet making the close friendships I so desperately craved. I was spending every weekend asleep on my sofa and watching movies in between. It took every ounce of energy to get up and go to work. I went to see a doctor, and he prescribed Prozac. It was a game changer. After a few weeks, my physician told me I was a different person. I took Prozac for about two years, until I had developed coping skills for being on my own and so far away from home.

Years later, once I was married, I began having those sinking feelings again. I felt like I had no hope. I was having minor panic attacks during the second year of my marriage. When I told my husband I was ill and asked him to stay with me, he called the neighbor. Shane asked Bonnie to come over and "keep an eye on me." The man who seldom worked had work to do.

When I wasn't hyped up and suffering from insomnia, all I wanted to do was stay in bed, under the covers, and hide from life. My counselor recommended that I see my family physician or a psychiatrist to be treated for anxiety and depression. It helped. Most of what I learned was that I wasn't crazy. Today, I continue to take a low dose of an antidepressant. It certainly helped me going through my divorce and managing the day-to-day stresses of raising a son on my own.

I am not recommending that you run out and ask for medication. Talk to a counselor first. Maybe talking it out is all you need. If that fails to bring you back to a healthier place, then medical intervention may help.

The main thing is, don't be embarrassed or ashamed. The Centers for Disease Control and Prevention say that eleven percent of the U.S. population takes an antidepressant. When you are ending or in the middle of a relationship with a narcissist, the stress you are under can feel insurmountable. Talk to your doctor and counselor. Make an informed decision.

It's difficult enough to function in an already busy and stressful society. Then, when you have a narcissist stealing your identity, self-worth, and any shred of self-esteem left, depression easily sets in. Keep in mind that the narcissist is also good at isolating her victims. Therefore, you don't have the support system from friends and family you need, either. If you or someone you know has symptoms of depression and anxiety, get help. Dr. Sawchuk says symptoms of both conditions usually improve with psychological counseling, medications such as antidepressants, or both. Lifestyle changes, such as improving sleep habits, increasing social support, using stress-reduction techniques or getting regular exercise, also may help. If you have either condition, avoid alcohol, smoking, and recreational drugs. They can make both conditions worse and interfere with treatment.

Reach out to your physician, counselor, good friend, or church mentor. People are ready to help point you in the right direction for treatment.

CHAPTER 12

Divorcing the Narcissist

Do not hold your breath for anyone,
Do not wish your lungs to be still,
It may delay the cracks from spreading,
But eventually they will.
Sometimes to keep yourself together
You must allow yourself to leave,
Even if breaking your own heart
Is what it takes to let you breathe.

– Erin Hanson

Saying Yes to a Different Fairy Tale: You

This wasn't the life or fairy tale you said "yes" to. And you long for it to return to the early days when you were swept off your feet and your significant other worshipped the ground you walked on. But remember, your fairy tale isn't coming back because it wasn't there in the first place. It wasn't real. Remember, it was all an act to hook you, before your partner changed into the "real" person you now see. It will break your heart. It can bring you to your knees. But, so would staying to endure decades more of abuse.

I am not advocating for divorce or saying it's easy. If there's one reason I stayed years more than I should have in my marriage, it was for my son. I wanted to have that quintessential family unit for my son. My dream was to have a family with a mother, father, child, and a dog. I wanted my team to do life together. If someone could've thrown in the white picket fence and a homemade pie cooling on the windowsill, I would've taken that, too. Unfortunately, my dream was a nightmare. It was time to wake-up and protect my son and myself.

If you are married to a narcissist, and you've realized she won't change, then you have a choice to make. You can divorce your narcissist or try to survive years more of manipulation and cruelty. I personally didn't want to spend the next thirty or forty years watching my back and never knowing what kind of chaos or toxic environment I was coming home to.

> *Remember, it was all an act to hook you, before your partner changed into the "real" person you now see.*

A woman who joined my Facebook group for victims and survivors of narcissistic abuse recently reached out to me. She has been married to a narcissist for forty-two years. It has taken her over four decades to realize that her husband will not change. She was further upset that he had put the blame on her for the dissolution of their marriage. (No surprise there. It's never the narcissist's fault.) He screamed at her, "You are going to let forty-two years go away like this? Poof and it's gone?" I encouraged her to remember that for forty years she had begged him to be nice, kind, and get help. It's not her. It's him. The saddest part for this woman is that she feels like she's wasted decades waiting for him to change.

During our divorce process, my ex first told me he was representing himself. Shane said he would not pay an attorney to do what he can do. "Laura, I am not going to stand in front of a judge and give an attorney thousands of dollars to do what I can do. You are being ridiculous. Let's just sit down, and if you come to your senses, you'll take the deal I am offering you."

My ex thought he could represent himself through the entire process. Never mind that he would be negotiating with attorneys who had graduated law school, clerked for federal judges, and served as family court judges. My ex still thought he knew more than they did. It was also a way to manipulate me.

Before he came to his senses, he offered me about ten percent of what we had accumulated during our thirteen years of marriage. Now I can laugh and think that I should have encouraged him to represent himself and let my attorney represent me. It would have been an entertaining debacle. But, as usual, he was being a bully and trying to pressure me into taking a minimal amount of assets and home equity, when I was the one who wanted only my son.

You cannot predict what your narcissist will do. You may feel like a moving target, unable to anticipate the narcissist's next move. But there are ways to make the impact of your divorce minimal.

Dennis Brewer was recently a partner in an award-winning Family Law firm in Grapevine, Texas. Dennis is now working full time at Fellowship Church in Grapevine, but graciously discussed his thirty years inside and outside the courtroom for this book. Dennis recommended the three types of approaches to divorce and what works better for victims and survivors of narcissistic abuse.

Brewer says to do these three things when first filing for a divorce:

1. **Choose the right attorney.** Brewer says to use referrals from trusted friends or family members, and then look for these things.

    a. Make sure the attorney is a board-certified specialist. This means that the attorney, in states like Texas, has practiced law for five years, has represented a plaintiff or defendant in a jury trial, and has done appellate work.

    b. Make sure the attorney has represented the victims, but also understands the "alphas" or narcissists.

2. **Trust your attorney. Let your attorney make the decisions.**

Brewer said, "You are coming from such a broken place that you will not make the right decisions. Typically, what you think is the right thing to so will not be the right thing to do. Narcissists have learned how to cover and manipulate you for so long, you won't know how to make every decision about your future correctly."

3. **Negotiate attorneys' fees. You can negotiate attorneys' fees up front with your attorney if the attorney agrees, or you can negotiate that your-soon-to-be ex will cover the lawyers' fees. But this needs to be discussed up front before the divorce process begins.**

Once you or your ex has filed for divorce, Brewer said to determine what process you want to use to divorce.

1. **Divorce in the court room: A trial by judge or jury. In most states and the overwhelming number of divorce**

cases, there is no jury trial. Instead, a single judge will preside over and decide an entire trial. This marks a major change in American law. Not even fifty years ago, many divorce trials were held before a jury. But now it would be comparatively rare for a jury to decide a Family Law case. Juries can be used in Texas and Georgia.

Brewer said that trials by judge or jury are very expensive. Witnesses must be prepared, jurors must go through voir dire, jury consultants may be hired, and evidence needs to be gathered.

Brewer said his experience with narcissists is that the people who want to go to trial are usually the narcissists.

"Those are the people you do not want to go to trial with," he added.

"It is a difficult thing to go through, it is expensive, it's risky. So no, your goal as a lawyer is to settle the case outside a trial setting."

Brewer said if you do go to trial, make sure your attorney knows or is familiar with the family court judges. The attorney needs to understand the ins and outs of a particular courtroom and Family Law. Make sure the attorney has tried a case in that court before.

> *Brewer said his experience with narcissists is that the people who want to go to trial are usually the narcissists.*

Leslie Brennan, a Family Law attorney in the Dallas area, recently posted recommendations about divorcing a narcissist on her website. She mentioned that narcissists will do anything to win. Although my ex wanted to avoid a trial, Brennan believes that many will prefer a court battle. She agrees with recent research published by *Psychology Today* that a narcissist may relish going to court and having a judge make the final decision. This may actually make the narcissist more comfortable because it means he or she doesn't have to take any responsibility for the outcome, especially if it's not favorable. Narcissists hate to lose, so if they can blame a loss on someone else, all the better.

The narcissist may want to engage you in a court battle so he can make it all about himself. When they have to respond to litigation from you, they take delight in that because they get to play the victim and seek attention from others who support their pity party.

IMPORTANT: Most attorneys will try to settle the divorce case before it reaches the point of a trial. Attorneys for each side negotiate all matters involved regarding the divorce, and then a decree is written up. Once both parties have agreed to every point in the decree and signed the decree, one or both parties must appear in front of a judge and the divorce is granted. Do this. Push for this. Don't engage in a trial or courtroom battle.

2. **Mediation:** A mediator sits down with both parties for the sole purpose of hammering out an agreement. There is no trial setting. Brewer says the mediator's sole purpose is to reach an agreement, regardless of the outcome or what is best for all parties involved. He says some will care how the case is settled, but that is how mediators make a living. They settle cases.

Brewer says, "Their job is to facilitate settlement. Period. What they think or what they believe is irrelevant. Their goal is quite frankly not trying to take care of your needs as a litigant, but their goal is to settle the case. That is a win for them."

Brewer also says, "Good attorneys will mediate anyway, as part of the process. A good attorney will try to keep the case out of the courtroom."

3. **Collaborative Law:** A somewhat new legal process in Family Law that insures the divorce will stay out of the courtroom if the process is followed through to its resolution. This method can enable couples who have decided to separate or end their marriage to work with their lawyers and, on occasion, other family professionals in order to avoid the uncertain outcome of court and to achieve a settlement that best meets the specific needs of the parties involved, including the children.

However, there is no courtroom discovery, and each party signs a document that agrees that party will turn over all pertinent financial information and other important information. This process relies on complete honesty on both sides of the divorce.

Brewer says stay away from collaborative law when you are divorcing a narcissist. He cites the fact there is no courtroom discovery or forensic accounting. (Forensic accounting is when an accountant specializing in money trails and records looks for any hidden assets that your ex is trying to cover up.) There is one expert who works for you both.

Brewer says, "It's a narcissist's or an alpha's dream to come to the table and snow everyone. You (the victim) are fodder in that situation."

During my divorce, I decided against collaborative law for the reasons Brewer recommends avoiding it. I knew from previous arguments with my ex that he was skilled at saying just the right things that would anger me, and then I would raise my voice and say "STOP IT." My ex would then calmly look at me and say "Why can't you talk about this like a sane, rational person? Don't you see that YOU'RE the problem here?"

I could see my ex falsely painting me as the crazy wife in the divorce process. I could almost hear him saying, "This woman has been given everything by me. I'm a kind, warm-hearted, Christian man who wants nothing but the best for my wife and son. And now look. She wants out. And I am left alone, as a bereft father."

CHAPTER 13

Preparing for Divorce: What to Do Now, Even If You Aren't Ready

What we wait around a lifetime for with one person, we can find in a moment with someone else.

– Stephanie Klein, *Straight Up and Dirty*

Here are my recommendations, and those of some attorneys, if you are thinking that divorce is an option. These worked for me, and perhaps you can take some or all of them for assistance in protecting yourself and your children.

1. Document. Document. Document.

Document everything. Start now, even if you are months or years away from getting a divorce. Whether it's in the notes section of your phone, on your computer, or in a written journal, record everything in writing. By the time I filed for divorce, I had recorded as many of the abusive incidents as I could. I even audibly recorded some on my phone that are saved to this day. Go as far back as you can remember and write the incidents down. If you can't remember the exact dates for your log, use an approximate date.

This documentation can be good for court cases, but mostly, it's good for your sanity. The gaslighting causes us to forget or gloss over reality. We don't want to remember the pain. But documentation can also provide clarity after you leave. Review the notes when you find yourself looking back on only the good times so you can remember the bad. ("Splitting" is the term used in psychology for looking at a relationship or situation in one way or through one lens. We will talk about this more when we discuss healing later in the book.) You'll look back and feel even more secure that you will NEVER go back to him. Or anyone like him. Celebrate your strength.

2.   Start meeting with attorneys.

Several Family Law attorneys will not charge a consultation fee. If there is a fee, look at it as an investment in your peaceful, happy future. Once you've consulted with an attorney, that attorney cannot work with your significant other.

Then, hire the best divorce attorney as you can afford. I worked with an attorney and his partners who are skilled at handling high-conflict divorces. The lead attorney was a former family court judge who knew the ins and outs of divorcing a narcissist. If you can't afford an attorney, many local colleges or universities offer free advice certain evenings or Saturdays so that law school students can gain experience. You never know how they can help you. They may put you in touch with a low-cost attorney or a lawyer who will take your case without money until the matter is settled. Be careful and negotiate a rate up front, though. You don't want to find yourself owing more than your divorce provides you.

3. Stay away from collaborative law.

I agree with Brewer's advice to stay away from collaborative law. Collaborative law is where both parties in the divorce (husband and wife) come to the table and negotiate what's best for all involved with an expert or mediator and both attorneys at the table. This process usually works well when there are kids involved and there are no psychological problems or personality disorders. A psychologist may evaluate all parties in the divorce proceedings, including the children. However, a narcissist is a skilled manipulator who may be able to influence this situation, too. A narcissist always is out for himself, so why would a divorce be any different?

I also knew that my life would be under a microscope and that my ex would try use my indiscretions against me. My attorney told me that there are sadly so many affairs today that most family court judges don't blink twice at news of an affair.

4. Make an interim plan, written or verbally, with the help of an attorney.

In Texas, there is no legal separation. Your state may have the same. You are either married or divorced. When divorce papers are filed, there is often an immediate need for a temporary order. Temporary orders are issued by a judge, and the orders decide who lives in the family home, how much each spouse will pay toward household bills, whether bank accounts and other assets are frozen and how time with any children is shared. In my case, my attorney did the work to draw up the temporary orders and then sent them to my ex's attorney for review and signatures. A court date is set in case both parties cannot agree on the temporary orders. At such a hearing, both sides present relevant testimony, and documents can be entered as evidence. I consider it a "mini-trial." The judge will hear testimony from witnesses and documents can be entered as evidence. What's presented in such hearing can later be used in the actual divorce trial, should there be one. If you need temporary orders, most attorneys agree this is a very important step in the divorce process. What is decided in the orders helps set the precedence for the divorce.

Keep in mind most temporary orders are signed by both parties and a court hearing isn't necessary. However, my ex had the temporary orders for approximately three weeks before our court date. As the date grew closer, I had to find friends who would testify for me in court about my parenting skills. Then those friends had to discuss and review their testimony with my attorney, who was charging me for that time.

I couldn't quit crying the morning of the hearing. I was terrified my ex would take me to court and convince the judge that I was an unfit mother. (I am a great mom, by the way. I am not close to perfect, but there is a lot of love and laughter and comfort in my home, especially now.) Three hours before our court appearance, my ex signed the papers. He made no changes. It was all a power struggle and a sick game for him. He knew he would sign the papers all along. He wanted to show me that he was in charge by having me anxiously wait and spend money that I didn't need to spend.

5. Ask the ex to leave the home, not you.

The first time I met with my attorney I wasn't quite ready to file for divorce. I met with him about nine months before I developed the courage. I knew I was headed in that direction, so I wanted to arm myself with the most information I could find. Sometimes these early meetings can be very informative and even free. My attorney advised me then that if I did decide to separate or divorce, to ask my husband to leave the family home. My attorney told me to under no circumstances to be the one to vacate the property. My lawyer said some judges don't like what appears to be abandonment of the family home.

I had heard from friends who had been in abusive marriages that they could look back to a specific day and time and tell you it was at that moment that they were ready to leave. I can say the same. It was a gorgeous Sunday afternoon in May 2015, and I was sitting by the window watching kids play in our backyard. My ex stopped by the table where I was checking email and accused me again of multiple affairs and boyfriends and hiding things. I said, "Ex, this is work email. You are welcome to take a look." He kept yelling. At that moment, as I watched my son laugh and play outside on what should be a relaxing, fun-filled Sunday afternoon, I knew I had hit my limit. I didn't need or have to live this way anymore. Immediately I looked at my husband, slammed my laptop shut, and said "Get out. I am done."

He smirked and rolled his eyes as if to say. "Well, we've been through this before. Whatever. You'll calm down."

I told him to pack for at least a week and to get out right now. I think he could sense the calm seriousness in my voice, for that was something I hadn't had before. He packed for a few nights away, thinking I would come to my senses. I went to visit with my attorney the next morning at 8 a.m. I told Larry, my attorney, "Let's do this. I am ready." My attorney filed the papers that very same Tuesday, and we had my ex served a few days later.

In some states, who vacates the marital home first is important to the courts. It's easier for the one who stays initially to have primary residence in the home as the temporary orders are issued.

Once the temporary orders were issued in our case, the court orders gave me some peace. I was to stay in the marital home with my son until the divorce was final. However, my ex was allowed in the home when he needed work documents or to see his son.

Here's where I initially made mistakes. My ex was ordered to give me a 24-hour notice that he was going to come inside the home. He usually gave 24 minutes, under the auspice that he "was in the neighborhood" and needed to stop by. I should have demanded him to follow the orders. At the time he was staying with a friend who lives 15 miles away. My ex knew my work schedule, so he would time it just right. While I was working, he would come into the office we shared and would rifle through documents, read my emails, and open my personal mail.

Don't let your ex bully you. Talk to your attorney so this doesn't happen to you. You don't want your soon-to-be-ex obtaining any personal information about you. That part of sharing those things is over and done. End of story.

6. Ask your attorney about changing the locks.

My ex had such a sense of entitlement that he would help himself to whatever was left in the home. My attorney said that since the temporary orders signed by the judge gave me the home as my primary residence, I could change the locks on the home. A-1 Locksmith couldn't get there fast enough. My attorney reminded me that I could unlock the home as long as I was provided with the 24-hour notice the temporary orders demanded.

Don't underestimate what your ex-partner will do. A narcissist feels entitled to everything. For example, I would find myself locked out of my bank account online as my ex had tried to access my bank account from the family computer. The bank had even issued a fraud alert. Change all your passwords, alarm codes, etc.

7. Find a friend to keep your important, most cherished assets or documents.

During my separation, I was out walking my cocker spaniel named Paris Hilton one afternoon in May. We had just separated that week. (Don't judge my dog. This dog was my best friend, born before my son. She was blonde, a diva, and I thought the name was cute and it fit.) I ran into a neighbor who I knew to be a kind person and a Christian woman. Michelle (we'll call her) asked me, "How are you?" I burst into tears and told her I had asked my husband to leave the house and I was filing for divorce. We stood in my driveway and cried for an hour. It was then that Michelle told me her mom had been married to an abuser and she understood what I was going through. She had witnessed it first-hand. Michelle encouraged me to get a lock box to keep at her house, and I could put important documents, pay stubs, bank statements, my engagement ring, and my grandmothers' jewelry there. I followed her suggestion that very afternoon. I knew not to put anything past my ex.

It turned out to be a smart move on my part. The next day my ex needed to get into the house to ostensibly search for some work documents. I found my jewelry box open and my personal belongings in a mess. My ex had rifled through my things, looking for ammunition or expensive belongings.

I encourage you, if you are leaving someone, to protect those things that are rightfully yours. Find a friend to keep your possessions. Narcissists consider themselves entitled to everything, even if you are leaving them or already divorced.

8. Look for proof of income.

I didn't do this and should have. Dig for proof of income. It saves money during the financial disclosure part of the proceedings. Many times you can spend thousands of dollars on the work of a forensic accountant to uncover the true assets of your spouse. Try to save yourself some money and take pictures of check stubs or bank statements. Ask your accountant for copies of the last five years of tax returns if you filed together. Get bank statements printed ASAP. The accounts could be locked down or frozen during proceedings.

9. Take pictures of the valuable possessions you cannot remove from the home.

You never know what can go missing. Take pictures of the items that mean the most to you. I didn't do this, and one of my favorite portraits of my son was "lost" when I moved out. I remember distinctly setting it in the office near the front door. That past summer, I had paid the photographer for a photo session with my son. The 11 x 14 print was expensive. My son told me recently that he's seen the picture hanging on the wall of his father's home, matted and framed.

10. Let the attorneys negotiate.

You are hiring them to fight for you, so let them do it. Give them all the information that you feel the need to give them, and then let them work. They can negotiate the best settlement for you. It's what you are paying them for, and it will keep you sane.

Your ex may try to talk you into meeting to discuss a division of property. Remember how skilled they are at manipulation. You don't want to do this. As soon as they get what they think they deserve, you might find yourself on the losing end, significantly.

11. Understand that the narcissist will likely use any children as pawns or part of the divorce game.

Narcissists want to win at any cost, and if you are a mother divorcing the narcissist, understand that most men know our children come first. They understand that's where they can get us to acquiesce to their demands, financial or otherwise. It might be that they fight for custody or possession of the children to simply hurt you. Or they may negotiate more money for themselves and give you more time with the children. The narcissist has not put his family first yet, so he won't do that during a divorce. Be careful and let your attorney know how your ex may play games.

One member of my Facebook group recently said that her ex-husband, a narcissist, filed a lawsuit to get full custody of their three children.

Until this point the custody had been about sixty percent-forty percent, with the mom having the children the majority of the time. This woman is a physician and one of the kindest people I've met. She dedicates her life to helping patients and curing illnesses. Her ex spoke to the children, methodically over time, about her mother having affairs (she didn't). He also accused this woman of physical abuse of one of her children. The case is still moving through the court system.

During my divorce process, my ex would reach out to me before contacting his attorney, trying to make "a deal." He threatened that he would fight for full custody of my son unless I took his offer of a minimal amount of money from him. I did ultimately settle for significantly less than 50% of marital assets so I could have primary possession of my child. My attorney advised me against this. We both knew my ex wasn't forthcoming about his finances. He was hiding money, but I was so hurt and done at this point I just wanted out. I wanted the pain to stop and no amount of money could trump that.

12. Don't worry about what people think.

The narcissist cares so much about perception and status that I am sure she has painted the picture of a perfect marriage and family for all to see. The narcissist will hate that facade coming to an end. Forget what others think and don't listen to what they say. You know what hell you've lived in. You are moving on. You will come out on top and have happiness and peace. Your inner circle will stand behind you. Those who don't, well, they don't deserve you anyway. I had one friend who cried when I told her I filed for divorce. She tried to talk me into staying with my ex. When I didn't, she soon distanced herself from me. My actions and decisions forced her to look in her mirror, and she doesn't like what she sees. Why? She's married to a narcissist. She's depressed, fractious, and constantly on edge as she tries her best to manage her toxic home life and two children. In these situations, I recommend praying for these men or women. Then move on. They may reach out to you one day when they've had enough. Or they may not. Pity them for that. But you have moved closer to finding your peace and purpose. There is so much you can have and deserve.

CHAPTER 14

After the Divorce: Breathe,
but Don't Take Off Your Armor

After your divorce, don't put anything past your ex. When you have left a narcissist, it's the injury you have inflicted that has the narcissist out for revenge, whether it's through money or the children.

My son and I had found a home in the same small city in the Dallas area where we lived as a family. I wanted to disrupt my son's life as little as possible. He could attend the same elementary school and church and have the same friends.

The unfortunate part was that the previous owner had cared for three long-haired, Persian cats. I am highly allergic to cat dander, so before we could officially move in, I had cleaners come three times to get it all. We were also redoing the floors the cats had destroyed, so my son and I couldn't officially move in for about three days past the day my divorce was actually final. I had asked my ex if we could stay in the family home for two nights until I could move in my home. He agreed to continue staying with a friend. However, the night the divorce was final, he barged in what was his home and demanded that he be there. He threw us out. He said, "Laura, you really went through with it so now you are on your own. Take these two damn dogs and get out."

I grabbed the remaining things that were left at the house, my son and the dogs, Paris and Joey, and shoved them into the car. We tried to sleep in sleeping bags on the floor of my new home in the one room that had new carpet and lacked cat dander. My son didn't like the smell of the new carpet, and he was scared of being in a house so empty of furniture. When tears began to fall down his face, around 1 a.m., we packed up again and went to a nearby Marriott Courtyard. This hotel didn't take dogs, but I was desperate. I'm embarrassed to say that my son and I snuck our two cocker spaniels into the hotel and had a few hours of sleep before vacating and heading to our new home.

This is where it grew comical. My good friend Amy says, "You just can't make this stuff up." As we were leaving the hotel around 6 a.m., I told my son to be careful, look both ways, and run to the car! He had Joey, and I had the sweet, docile Paris. Well, Joey loved me, his mama. Joey wasn't going anywhere if I was down the hall without him. I remember that black-and-white spotted dog craning around the corner of the hallway, while I simultaneously heard the hotel manager coming from the other direction. I said, "Go, son, go!" To this day, I can see Joey's head as he leaned around the corner, before my son yanked him off his four paws. It was as if he was being pulled of the stage with a giant cane. That poor dog flew through the air with a loud "AAARRFFFFF." So, yes, the hotel manager caught us, wagging tails and all, and I had to pay the $100 pet fee. We boarded the dogs the next day and found a hotel for one more night until our new home was ready.

The Children

> There is no such thing as a "broken family." Family is family, and is not determined by marriage certificates, divorce papers, and adoption documents. Families are made in the heart. The only time family becomes null is when those ties in the heart are cut. If you cut those ties, those people are not your family. If you make those ties, those people are your family. And if you hate those ties, those people will still be your family because whatever you hate will always be with you.
>
> – C. Joy Bell

It goes without saying that you need to make sure your children are okay after the divorce. It's imperative that they have an open line of communication with you at all times, whether at your home or that of your former partner.

Dr. Ray Levy, a therapist in Dallas, Texas, believes how you tell children about the upcoming divorce is one of the most important things you will do in the divorce process.

"Children I have worked with all remember certain events on certain says, and where they were when those events happened," Dr. Levy said. "We can all remember where we were when we heard about 911. This isn't any different. Most of the children in my practice can tell me exactly where they were when they were told their parents were divorcing."

Dr. Levy recommends that you talk to your counselor about the best way to tell your children, or you pick up a book on divorce and its effects on kids. There are even books that give your scripts of how to tell children about the divorce.

Dr. Levy also says to get the kids in counseling. I had my son in counseling the week his dad moved out. It was expensive, but the returns are priceless. We are shaping the next sixty to seventy years of life for these children. When professional counseling can help, let it.

Also, talk about the divorce with them. Tell them how much you love them and that the divorce is not their fault. I told my son that his father and I love him so very much, but we love him better when we are apart. I also did my daily check-in. I would say, "Buddy, how are you feeling today? What are you thinking about as far as our new life goes?" In the beginning he would tell me his feelings; then it got to the point that he was entrenched in our new life and his new friends, and he'd answer, "Mom, I AM FINE. Would you please quit asking me that silly question? I KNOW the divorce isn't my fault."

> *I had my son in counseling the week his dad moved out. It was expensive, but the returns are priceless.*

Nevertheless, I still check in with him from time to time.

When my ex and I were still married, there were a few years near the end of our marriage when stomach pains would leave my sweet child doubled over in pain. Physicians at Dallas Children's Medical Center evaluated him from head to toe, and completed numerous scans including an endoscopy. They found nothing physically wrong. After the divorce, interestingly, my son's stomach pains resolved. I believe moving out of the toxic environment was good for my son and myself.

If you have joint custody or shared custody of any type, I learned that it was best to communicate all issues regarding child care over email. That way there is a written trail. There are also apps that can serve as the communication tool between you and your ex. Anything communicated in this app can be used as evidence, should you need to go to court again.

Leopards and Your Ex: Neither Changes Spots

Don't' expect your ex to change after the divorce. She will still be deceitful and selfish, even with items that are yours. I expected mine to finally come to his senses and realize that I obviously wasn't backing down and maybe even apologize. I expected him to become civil and lose his sense of entitlement to everything that was mine. Boy was I wrong. With a narcissist, it's not going to happen. Ever. They are always right.

Right after our divorce, I had ordered some tickets to see my favorite country artist, Kenny Chesney. Stub Hub accidentally sent the tickets to my old address. My ex signed for them when they came by Fed Ex. I was so disappointed. I wanted to go to the concert and besides, I had spent a lot of money on these tickets!

I called my ex the next day and said, "Hey there. I need you to give me back the Kenny Chesney tickets. They came to your front door."

"Tickets? What tickets, Laura?" he said. "I haven't been home in a while."

He was blatantly lying to me. "I don't have the tickets."

> *They will feel slighted after a divorce, so do not put anything past them.*

I reminded him that opening someone else's mail can be a federal offense, and that he needed to return my Fed Ex envelope to my house by 6 a.m. the next day or I was calling the police. Around 2:30 a.m. I heard a car door slam. My ex had left the tickets in a new Fed Ex envelope. I could tell he had cut the label off the old envelope, put the tickets inside a new envelope, and attached the old label. He thought I wouldn't notice the tampering. He wanted to take a date to the concert, using my expensive tickets.

Even recently, my pet sitter and I have noticed that my things aren't always in their proper place when I come home from day trips or overnight trips for work. My son has let me know that sometimes "Dad doesn't follow your rules, Mom. He likes to come in the house and look around."

Install cameras. Ask for police patrols. The true narcissist has such a serious sense of entitlement that she may even break in to your home to get a glimpse into your new life. They want to see how you are doing so they can criticize it or make themselves feel better. They will feel slighted after a divorce, so do not put anything past them. I've had to call the police twice and file reports, and I've threated to call the authorities many other times. Your property is not the property of your ex. Even if she shows up and is yelling and calling you names without any physical abuse, still call law enforcement. It creates a paper trail and shows her you mean business.

Today, my security cameras and alarm system are mounted by each door to my home. The police first get a call if the alarm is activated, and then the cameras alert me. Trust me, my ex would come in uninvited every time if he could. In fact, he's never been invited. I don't trust him. I never will.

Yes, my house is smaller, but it is so full of love and laughter I wouldn't trade my house for anything. Our home is the place where middle-school boys come to play Xbox, eat me out of house and home, and play with our dogs. It is so much fun.

Money and Child Support

In Texas, the attorney general's office takes child support out of a father's pay and transfers it to the other parent, typically the mother. This can be reversed when the mother is the primary breadwinner. By having the state involved with payments, this keeps the fighting at a minimum when the payments aren't on time. The Office of the Attorney General will not put up with delinquent payments in the state of Texas. Offenders can be arrested.

Don't expect your ex to split things evenly or share expenses that aren't outlined in the decree. The ex may give you the sob story or promise that she will help with expenses, but if it's not in writing, don't expect it to happen. Often, my ex won't even feed my son dinner when I ask him to grab a sandwich for our twelve-year-old on the way home from basketball. That's extra money he feels entitled to keep for himself.

My friends who have been through a divorce and share costs for sports or piano lessons, find that a third bank account used solely for that purpose works well. For example, if Courtney needs money for the soccer fees from her ex, he puts the $50 in the joint account. Then Courtney can withdraw it after paying the soccer fees in full. This works for some. There is a paper trail for the court system, too.

Friends

You may still have some friends left from your pre-divorce life. Those who don't support you? Let. Them. Go.

I cannot say it enough. It is crucial to surround yourself with people who believe in you and your decision. There are still some friends today who say they "feel sorry" for me. Let me tell you something: There is no reason to feel sorry for me. That was hands down the best decision I ever made. If you tell a friend that, and they still criticize your choice or look down on you, it's because they are most likely in a painful marriage themselves and aren't as strong as you. Or, they selfishly want you and the ex as another couple to do things with. Or, maybe they don't believe in divorce. Regardless, these aren't true friends. Don't waste another minute of your precious time coddling them, appeasing them, or explaining it to them. They don't deserve it.

> *Regardless, these aren't true*
> *friends. Don't waste another*
> *minute of your precious time*
> *coddling them, appeasing*
> *them, or explaining it to them.*
> *They don't deserve it.*

Pastor Ed Young said in a recent sermon that he has had thousands of haters over the last 28 years. "Do not respond to the haters," Pastor Young said. "Hey student. Hey guy or girl addicted to social media. Don't respond to the haters. Jesus didn't. Your friends don't need an explanation. And your enemies won't believe it even if you give them one. So, I want to sit by the river long enough and watch my critics float by."

And you WILL watch new friends float into your life. As you get your old self back and develop your new self, you will meet nice, kind people. I've met many great friends, and two are extra special to me. One is married and one is divorced. We travel with and without kids to places all over the country and world. We laugh, we cry, and we love each other. We can call each other anytime about anything, and there is no judgment! They are the best friends I could ever have! They are my tribe. Find your tribe. You are ready to have an army that loves you.

CHAPTER 15

Healing: The Most Important Part of the Rest of Your Life

Relationships with narcissists are held in place by hope of a "someday better," with little evidence to support it will ever arrive.

– Ramani Durvasula, Should I Stay or Should I Go? Surviving a Relationship with a Narcissist

The first Christmas Eve as a single mother after my divorce found me curled up in a ball in the corner of my bedroom, sobbing. I couldn't believe things had turned out this way. I felt like I had destroyed my son's life and lost my dream of the family unit, all because I couldn't survive one more day of abuse. A broken heart, especially one from a codependent relationship, can bring you to your knees. The only time I wasn't in pain was when I was asleep. And some days I woke up wishing I were dead.

Then came the questions to myself. Should I have been stronger? Should I have tried to tough it out longer, just in case he would change? Deep down I understood, however, that I had to press on. My son and I could find happiness. I knew I couldn't give up. We could build a life that was happier than it ever had been. My family unit didn't have to be the father-mother-child entity.

Remember that everyone is hurting. Part of the human experience is pain. One of my favorite pastors, Dharius Daniels, says, "As long as we continue to breathe, we will continue to feel pain." Therefore, we need to heal. It's an ongoing process.

> *It's not your fault they hurt you, but it's your responsibility to heal. No one is coming to save you.*
> *– Rebecca Lynn Pope*

There are different levels of healing. Right now, your level of healing is high and crucial, but completely possible. Divorce, or a breakup, or simply walking away from someone you love in your life is difficult enough. But when you have suffered narcissistic abuse, it's a dangerous place to be in and it's vital that you heal.

> *A broken heart, especially one from a codependent relationship, can bring you to your knees.*

This is the part of the book that I am so excited about, because there is hope for you and anyone who has been broken by narcissistic abuse. I turned to the experts to get their take on what healing looks like and the best approaches for anyone who has suffered from narcissistic abuse. I didn't include specific action steps to take, because I want you to work with a counselor or therapist and find YOUR best plan. And remember, you cannot do it alone. A self-help book would encourage you to look inward and try to heal on your own. There will be plenty of introspection. You need someone to listen and walk through this journey with you. It will go more quickly, and you will have others to lean on.

Spiritual Healing

Everyone's journey through life, and healing, is different. There is no magic path that will lead you to the "aha" moment where you hear a church choir sing and you proclaim, "I am HEALED!" But being healed is possible, and your healing is closer than you think.

I worked with counselors and church mentors for years. All served an important, and in the case of my eating disorder, life-saving and life-changing part of my healing. We will look at the different ways cognitive therapy can help as this chapter unfolds. But first, I want to explore spiritual healing. Before you shut this book, hear me out. Spiritual healing can be the icing on the cake or the last drop in a bucket that you need to move your healing along quickly. This healing is meant to be done in addition to cognitive or behavioral therapy, support groups, and other methods of healing.

Spirituality has become more popular in the last decade. Many women or men approach spirituality through religion, meditation, and personal reflection. The practice of spirituality is now recognized by some psychologists as an adjunct to a patient's cognitive therapy.

Dr. Ryan Howell, Associate Professor of Psychology at San Francisco State University, researched spirituality in 2013. He collected data from his website BeyondthePurchase.org. The questions on his website explored whether money can indeed buy happiness. He and his research team examined participants' responses to over thirty surveys. Dr. Howell found that the following are the top five characteristics of spiritual people.[37]

Spiritual people are gracious. Psychology has demonstrated that expressing gratitude is associated with many positive emotions such as optimism, being generous with time and resources, and overall vitality.

Spiritual people are compassionate. Experiencing compassion toward others is one the strongest correlates with living a spiritual life. A variety of positive or pro-social emotions have strong links with spiritualism, including allowing one to feel good about the little things in life and look at the world through empathetic eyes.

Spiritual people flourish. Spirituality is linked to many important aspects of human functioning: Spiritual people have positive relationships, high self-esteem, are optimistic, and have meaning and purpose in life.

Spiritual people self-actualize. Spiritual individuals strive toward a better life and consider personal growth and fulfillment as a central goal. Spirituality can be considered to be a path toward self-actualization, because it requires people to focus on their internal values and work on becoming a better individual.

Spiritual people take time to savor life experiences. Individuals who value spirituality take the time to reflect on their daily activities and ultimately build lasting memories of their experiences. Because spiritual people are more conscious of small, daily activities, they experience positive emotions associated with the smaller pleasures in life.

Rebecca Lynn Pope

When I needed and craved the final part of my healing process, I turned to Rebecca Lynn Pope. I was fortunate to find a mention of her on Twitter when she was asked to speak at Bishop T.D. Jakes' yearly "Mega Fest" in Dallas. The tweet caught my eye because Bishop Jakes mentioned how

Rebecca led a discussion to a packed house of men and women about dating in a Christian world. Bishop Jakes said she clearly explained why we can attract the wrong partners. It was like a dozen light bulbs went off in my head.

Rebecca is a Spiritual Healer, Counselor, and Life Coach. She's even done some matchmaking, but she will tell you that's not where her heart lies. Why? Because she believes most people don't heal the way they need to heal before dating or developing a relationship. Then, then the cycle starts all over again.

A major TV network approached Rebecca recently about a matchmaking show, and Rebecca declined the offer. Her purpose is in helping people recover from the death of a loved one, spiritual abuse, narcissistic abuse, and divorce. Rebecca was pivotal in my healing process. She's the main reason I am writing this book. Rebecca wants to give a voice and a face to this madness called narcissistic abuse.

Rebecca was brought up as a pastor's daughter in Ohio. Her father often turned to her to help others in the church heal when she was a young child. She has a gift for recognizing pain and helping others find help and healing and come out on the other side. She's written a book called *Love and Dating in the 20th Century*, in which she outlines her own painful past. She details mistakes and choices she made before taking a path to a healed life. She lives in Atlanta now with her husband, also a pastor, and spends her purpose-driven life healing and helping others.

Rebecca says healing is a process, and it takes several different forms of help to heal. "Very few people can heal in isolation," she says. "Renewing your mind and healing is all a process and no two journeys will look the same."

She recommends cognitive therapy, spiritual healing, and emotional healing as part of this process to a healed and happy life. Rebecca has worked with dozens of women and men who have suffered narcissistic abuse. Most of her clients have been in relationships with narcissists for at least ten years, while several others stayed in a toxic relationship for over twenty years. All her clients coming out of narcissistic abuse have stayed in such a partnership for one reason: hope that it will go back to what it was like in the beginning.

Rebecca calls these "soul ties." It's codependency. Lots of victims get out of a toxic relationship and get right back in. Victims are brainwashed to believe they can't do better or make it without this person. This, Rebecca says, is some of the most detrimental thinking. So, whether you've left the narcissist, or you are contemplating a departure, it's time to begin to heal. It's time to make a change and start a journey to a better life.

Here's her outline to grow from victim to survivor:

1. **Recognize that you've been in a relationship with a narcissist.**

    Many men and women aren't even aware that their partner, parent, or friend is a narcissist. They understand they've suffered some type of emotional and verbal abuse, but they didn't know how bad it was, nor can they articulate it well. Narcissistic abuse fits in an entirely different category.

    "I can counsel and help someone heal who's been through a divorce, but narcissistic abuse is an entirely different category," she says. "The biggest issue is that the narcissist has programmed the victim to turn on themselves, when it's not their fault."

    Rebecca says recognize that this isn't who you are but that this is something that's been done to you. Understand that you were the selected target because of the narcissist. It wasn't anything you did except be an empathic person or an empath.

"The biggest shocker I've seen is that narcissists will consistently find the people they are able to do the most damage on," she says. "They specifically prey on the sweetest, kindest people you have ever met."

2. Admit you are hurt and get intentional about healing.

Go after healing like you have gone after parenting, a new job, or the extra money you want to earn. Seek help. Healing requires intention. It's not going to fall in your lap or just happen. Don't expect a new relationship to heal you or make the pain go away.

"A new husband or wife or partner or friend isn't going to make the pain go away," Rebecca said. "That's just a Band-Aid and your wounds will bleed through."

Also, don't expect to heal in isolation. Very few people can heal in isolation. You need accountability. A life coach or counselor can help with that.

Finally, don't be embarrassed about admitting that you need healing. Rebecca says we all need healing throughout our lives, and many times this healing is at different levels. Coming out of a divorce or a narcissistic relationship, it's crucial to heal.

3. Develop an action plan.

Decide who fits best in your action plan for healing. There are many choices:

a. Counselor or therapist (cognitive therapy): These are usually PhDs or Licensed Clinical Social Workers who specialize in cognitive therapy or "talk" therapy. For me this was instrumental to my healing.

b. Spiritual healer: Someone who works with your spiritual energy or your belief in God to help find the path that fits your heart and mind and body. I have a friend who believes in Reiki therapy. The woman feels her energy as she passes her hands over my friend's body and uses her positive energy to heal my friend.

c. Minister: A church leader, pastor, or mentor who can listen and advise. Be careful you don't find too much judgment in the one you choose. You want someone who listens and can advise without judging your decisions.

d. Life coach: These are usually certified men or women who coach you through problems, choices, and outcomes as they relate to jobs, relationships, families, money, and more.

e. Support groups: There are groups for men and women who have been in abusive relationships, whether physical, mental, or both. Some victims I've spoken with continue to attend their AA meetings and find the support they need there while healing from narcissistic abuse. After all, in some cases, it was the abuse that caused them to choose alcohol as an escape from the pain.

f. Family physician: Your doctor can help steer you in a good direction for counseling or if you need medication for depression or anxiety.

g. Family and friends: These are family and friends who support you and your choice to leave the narcissist 100%. They don't question you. They let you talk it out as much as you need to, knowing that the more you vent, the better and more quickly you will heal. Leave any friend or family member who doesn't support you, or criticizes you, out of your support system. Understand that is not their place or their honor to be in your tribe. They may not be healed or may not believe you. It doesn't matter. Leave them out of these conversations. I've ended some friendships due to the lack of support or understanding. One couldn't love at my level so said goodbye. She was hypercritical, and it was always about her. Sound familiar? It was much too familiar to me to continue this friendship. I didn't need her criticism or neediness. It was time to put me first and she wasn't helping me do that. So, I said goodbye.

As Rebecca recommends to all her clients, everything you choose from here on out must be a part of the fundamental belief that you will heal. It will come down to this: Self-love. You will develop an unfaltering belief in yourself. You must come first.

Have patience with yourself. Healing takes time. Don't compare your journey to anyone else's. We all heal differently, depending on how you were raised, how much abuse you've been through, and how you internalize things. Your journey is special and unique, just like you are. You are stronger than you know. Look at what you've already survived.

Cognitive Therapy

Cognitive therapy is based on the cognitive model, which states that thoughts, feelings, and behavior are all connected, and that individuals can move toward overcoming difficulties and meeting their goals by identifying and changing unhelpful or inaccurate thinking, problematic behavior, and distressing emotional responses. This involves the individual working collaboratively with the therapist to develop skills for testing and modifying beliefs, identifying distorted thinking, relating to others in different ways, and changing behaviors. The therapist often helps the patient develop an action plan to counteract previous thinking and mindset. In many cases, it's an effective part of healing.

My initial healing began 25 years ago when I met Dr. Ray Levy, the psychologist I credit with saving my life. When you get down to 89 pounds at 5'6", you are certainly closer to death then you should be in your late teen years. The more therapy I had, the more I realized what growing up with a narcissistic parent had done to my psyche. I no longer needed to be her clone or her mini-me. I could be Laura.

> *He encouraged me not to call it not selfish behavior to put myself first, but to label self-care as self-preservation or self-love.*

Later, Dr. Levy helped me get through my divorce. He taught me that it's fundamental to put my happiness first. He encouraged me not to call it not *selfish* behavior to put myself first, but to label self-care as *self-preservation* or *self-love*. My pivotal point of therapy came when I realized I needed to be strong to raise my son into the smart, kind, Christian man I want him to be. If I couldn't take care of my emotional needs, I certainly couldn't take care of his.

There are many types of counseling you can try, and many types of counselors. I encourage you to ask friends you admire or trust for recommendations. Then, the most important part is to make sure the counselor has some experience in working with narcissists and their victims. You want a man or woman that understands the toxic, manipulative world you live in. Will he or she be able to give you concrete steps to survive? Is the counselor accessible for you during emergencies? If or when you leave your narcissist, you will need friends and counselors to be there when situations arise.

Energy Healing

There is a newer group of techniques that therapists often label Energy Healing techniques. The thought behind these techniques is that energy, or memories, often get stuck in parts of our brain that can't be reached with cognitive or talk therapy alone. Three of these techniques often used are EFT, EMDR, and hypnosis. I successfully used EFT and hypnosis as a patient of Dr. Levy, before, during, and after my dedication to healing began.

EFT (Emotional Freedom Technique)

EFT is the acronym for Emotional Freedom Technique. It has been used successfully with soldiers who suffer from posttraumatic stress disorder (PTSD). When I learned this, I was shocked to hear that narcissistic abuse was finally recognized by psychologists to be traumatic. I had lived it and believed it, but I was encouraged that therapists understood the damage, too.

EFT involves the therapist tapping on the forehead, arms, clavicle, and each shoulder as you relive traumatic events. You go through the events one by one, envisioning them, and then take your mind to a safe place, take a deep breath, and say "peace." After each session of painful memories, the last cycle of EFT involves replacing the painful thoughts with healed, positive ones.

Dr. Levy says the theory behind EFT is that it accesses painful memories buried in your subconscious. Those memories are the ones that are difficult to replace or analyze in talk therapy.

"It's a back door approach to the memories we can't access otherwise," Dr. Levy said. "We override the conscious mind which won't usually allow access. Then, in talk therapy, those memories can be addressed and put in their proper place in a patient's life."

For example, one of my best EFT sessions happened right after my divorce. Dr. Levy started by asking me questions about my pain from my ex moving on so quickly. I knew he was dating, and I was fearful he would replace me with someone better, smarter, and prettier. I had the irrational thought that he would find someone who would change him. She may be wife number four, but I was convinced she would get the best of what I never received from my ex.

My EFT session went something like this:

Dr. Levy began tapping.

"You know, Laura, your ex is going to go find the most beautiful woman to replace you. She's going to be gorgeous and smart, and your ex will give her everything he never gave you. He will finally change. You just aren't good enough to change him."

Meanwhile, I cried and cried.

Dr. Levy continued, "It's like you've always thought, Laura. You just aren't good enough. You aren't worth it. You aren't enough."

Then he would ask me to go to my safe place. My safe place many times during EFT was a hot summer day, riding horses behind one of my favorite people, a former U.S. Marshal. I could smell the horses, hear the hooves, and see the gun (for snakes) tucked into the jeans of my buddy.

I could hear the horses neigh as we slowly climbed up a cliff in the Texas Hill Country.

EFT helped me replace the beliefs I had developed through the abuse with positive affirmations and feelings. I learned that I am enough, I am worthy of love, and I am deeply loved. It sounds trivial to me as I write this, but when you are a shell of the person you once were, you will try anything to get that person back.

I've probably had about ten EFT sessions over the last five years. Each time it brought me further along than ten sessions of therapy did. EFT takes the painful memories, lets you process them differently, and then file them away somewhere else other than your subconscious. Dr. Levy compared it to moving things around on your desk and filing away what you don't need anymore.

Dr. Levy has seen significant results from abuse victims, including a rape victim who was able to move past the memories and continue to heal. He does recommend that it be used in conjunction with cognitive or talk therapy. He says after the memory is "unstuck," cognitive therapy is more effective and beneficial.

EMDR (Eye Movement Desensitization Technique)

The second technique some psychologists use as part of energy healing is called Eye Movement Desensitization Technique (EMDR). This therapy was also designed to alleviate the distress associated with traumatic memories.

EMDR is a longer process, but results have been significant. The EMDR Institute describes it likes this:

> Repeated studies show that by using EMDR therapy people can experience the benefits of psychotherapy that once took years to make a difference. It is widely assumed that severe emotional pain requires a long time to heal. EMDR therapy shows that the mind can in fact heal from psychological trauma much as the body recovers from physical

trauma. When you cut your hand, your body works to close the wound. If a foreign object or repeated injury irritates the wound, it festers and causes pain. Once the block is removed, healing resumes. EMDR therapy demonstrates that a similar sequence of events occurs with mental processes. The brain's information processing system naturally moves toward mental health. If the system is blocked or imbalanced by the impact of a disturbing event, the emotional wound festers and can cause intense suffering. Once the block is removed, healing resumes. Using the detailed protocols and procedures learned in EMDR therapy training sessions, clinicians help clients activate their natural healing processes.

The HMO Kaiser Permanente funded a study that found that 100% of the single-trauma victims and 77% of multiple trauma victims no longer were diagnosed with PTSD after only six 50-minute sessions. In another study, 77% of combat veterans were free of PTSD in 12 sessions.[38]

For more information about EMDR treatment of abuse victims, ask your therapist for guidance.

Hypnosis

Dr. Levy used hypnosis with me a few times to overcome extreme sadness I felt after my divorce. I knew I had made the right decision, but I was still mourning the divorce and the loss of my dream of a "family."

We may think of cartoons with someone waving a pocket watch saying "you are getting very, very sleepy." But that's not hypnosis at all. Have you ever been watching the car in front of you as you are driving, know where you are driving, but your mind is partially working out something else? That's what hypnosis is. A hypnotized person enters a highly alert state in which the person's focus or concentration is even more intense. A hypnotized person is also relaxed, allowing his mind to be open to suggestions to other ways of thinking. The conscious mind cannot fight the effort to retrieve a painful memory from the subconscious, and then replace it with a peaceful memory or belief.

Hypnosis can work because it allows patients to focus and sustain concentration, so they can be taught a well-thought-out behavior modification program. Dr. Levy taught me, through hypnosis, to make my divorce seem like a tiny pinprick of light in a tunnel, getting smaller and smaller. I had previously felt like my divorce was a freight train giving me only minutes to live before it ran me over. I am serious here. I pictured a huge light in a tunnel, then a smaller, almost tiny light by the end of my hypnotherapy sessions. Both lights symbolized my divorce: At first it was this huge glow, blinding me, knocking me off balance. Then, I learned to look at it like a small glow, a fading light of pain, loneliness, and abuse.

> *Meeting other kids whose parents have divorced has helped my son understand that he is not alone.*

Most psychologists say hypnosis should be viewed as an adjunctive part of an ongoing therapeutic plan. You can ask your counselor or get on the *Psychology Today* website to look for hypnotists in your area. I certainly would ask your counselor first.

Healing for Children
During this healing process, don't forget about your children. They need healing, too

There are so many good counselors out there that deal with divorce and narcissistic parents every day. Ask friends whose kids have seen a good one. Ask your counselor about a referral.

Many children like to have their own counselor and safe place, so that's why my son sees one on his own. My son thinks his counselor, Dr. Koy Roberts, is "cool." I appreciate Dr. Roberts' demeanor, candor, and expertise. Dr. Roberts specializes in adolescent boys, so there's an added perspective from someone who hears from teenage boys for hours each day. After my son finishes his session, Dr. Roberts fills me in on what we need to work on at home, such as firmer discipline, more encouragement, and curtailing behaviors that aren't age appropriate.

There are also support groups or classes for children that often coincide with Divorce Recovery or Divorce Care classes for adults. I know our church holds at least one class for kids each year. Meeting other kids whose parents have divorced has helped my son understand that he is not alone.

In almost any divorce situation, there is a tendency to overcompensate for the split. I have done this, and it's a daily struggle for me. Guilt and shame for staying in a toxic relationship are so strong that it's easy to spoil children and let them get away with behaviors you otherwise wouldn't tolerate. We need to be careful not to create "entitled little monsters," as Pope puts it.

Pope recommends that the best thing you can do for you children is:

1. **Evolve into a healthy person.**

> Remember that a healthy mom or dad is a better parent. A healed parent is the best parent. If you are a well-balanced mom who takes care of herself, demonstrates self-love, and embraces self-care, then you can have more kindness, boundaries, and patience.

2. **Find help for your child.**

Find a counselor for your children. Let them talk to you without judgment or taking it personally. They are like adults trapped in a little body. They have feelings and fears like we do. You don't want them internalizing, either.

Personally, I overcompensated out of guilt and shame for the divorce. Once we moved into our own home, there was little that I said "no" to or didn't buy for him. If I could afford it, he would get the latest X-box game or toy. I let him have sleepovers with multiple friends that would keep us all up most of the night. When I realized it was doing more harm than good, I stopped the indulgent pacification.

Three years later, we are both still in counseling as the need arises. Middle school has not been a simple transition for my son (or me). Working full time, raising a son, and managing a home on my own sometimes leaves me exhausted and prone to less patience and more criticism. I go to counseling as part of my self-care routine. I find that if I get "all up in my feelings" or overthink situations, I fall into negative thought patterns. And that doesn't do anyone any good.

My son sees his counselor every two weeks. It gives him a safe place where he can talk about school peer pressure and "boy stuff." The counselor gives me feedback and encouragement as we enter these 'tween and teen years. It also gives us both accountability to do what's right. I do my best to make sure I balance motherly love with proper discipline. And my son has to balance respect for our home rules, his needs, and his desires.

Dating Again

Healing before dating is essential, according to Rebecca Lynn Pope. She's seen bad experiences play out time and time again if a person dates and gets into a relationship before healing.

I wasn't ready to date right away. My counselor advised me against it until I felt a little stronger. I couldn't predict when the tears would come. I could be standing in line at the grocery store, working out at the gym, or singing songs in church, and they would just start flowing. I could become the caricature of a teenage drama queen in twenty seconds or less. You will mourn, even though your relationship was toxic.

> *"At the end of the day, when you aren't healed, you are wearing pain goggles."*
> *-Rebecca Lynn Pope*

But be ready: The narcissist needs his or her supply. And they'll need it right away. My ex started dating immediately. He let mutual friends know he was out almost every night. I also knew this because he would send me pictures of women and tell me he had upgraded. They were all beautiful women, usually with large breasts, short dresses, and lots of makeup. It was devastating to hear and see that he was moving on so quickly. But I kept reminding myself that he wouldn't change. He was someone else's problem now. Let her deal with it. I was free.

Dr. Ray Levy recommends that you can go out and have fun with people who might be a partner one day, but don't get in a relationship. You may feel ready, but you aren't. If you have done all this work to leave an abusive relationship with a narcissist, why would you want to do it all over again?

Pope recommends healing before dating for that reason. She says, "At the end of the day, when you aren't healed, you are wearing pain goggles. You see everything through a hurting cloud. Your vision isn't clear. Which means you could meet a really great person and tell yourself, 'No, I'm good. He or she is weird, and certainly not for me.'"

However, that person may be a great man or woman you just passed by because you are used to being in a relationship with someone who is broken and unhealed. Perhaps you are used to a narcissist. You are still more comfortable around the man who brags about himself, likes to be the center of attention, displays charisma, and makes you feel like a princess. You still don't see that underneath that mound of whipped cream, he is a bowl of poison.

Pope reminds us that when we are unhealed and trying to date, "You meet the mild-tempered, kind, sweeter man and you tell yourself, hmmm...I don't know about him. He seems weak. I want a manly man. I want a boss."

However, when you are healed, you "take off the pain goggles and your vision clears. Your spirit is free, and you meet this wonderful man who is sweet, kind, and mild tempered and all you feel is peace. Your peace resonates with his peace and you are like wow, you are amazing."

I have met several good men since my healing process began. In fact, for about eight months, I dated a wonderful man who loves me and my son. Recently, and unfortunately, we've agreed that he needs to have more healing in his life. A job loss, a divorce a year ago, and some health problems have him at his lowest low. He's not making good choices for his children or our relationship. He's seeing a counselor now, and he plans to work with Pope when it's financially easier for him. We are at such different places, our relationship is on hold. Am I crushed? No, but I am sad. I do have a sense of peace about this, too, that comes with being on my healing journey. I know God has a plan and a man for me, and I hope it's this one. But if not, I know I will be okay. I am happy and at peace with Laura. I don't take failed relationships as a sign that something is inherently wrong with me. It's either not the right time, or it's simply not right. Regardless, I will continue to live a life of peace, purpose, and love. A year ago I would've been destroyed. Now, I know I'll be okay.

Let the Healing Begin: You Will Find Your Joy!
The path you choose is up to you. But it must be intentional. Make your action plan and take the first step toward peace and happiness.

As you begin to find yourself, you'll rediscover old parts of you that have been dormant for some time or parts that need nurturing. Maybe you used to enjoy painting, jogging, or volunteering at a homeless shelter. Do it again. Do you like massages? Mani-pedis? Go get one occasionally. Treat yourself. Love yourself this way. Do something for *you* that you enjoy.

> *Get your joy back. There's no longer anyone there telling you that you can't do something or putting you down for even trying.*

You may also learn things about yourself that you didn't know can bring you joy. Maybe you want to try a new church or join a cycling group. My son and I now love the water. We bought a pre-owned wakeboard boat on *Boat Trader* last year, and we cannot wait for summer to use it again. It's ironic we've found this fun because the times on the "family" ski boat were so miserable. It's a delightful experience now. My son and his middle school buddies choose the music. It's usually rap or country which they play so loud I am sure it's heard all the way to Oklahoma. I drive. (You wouldn't believe how many men can't believe that a *woman* drives a *boat*. Um, is there a law somewhere that says only men can do this?) We spill Cheetos all over the boat. We laugh. We often bet a soda or ice cream bar on who will be knocked off the tube first each time. (It's this funny kid named Ryan. He's a goner after 20 yards on the tube. He just can't hang on.)

My point is, do what you love to do. Get your joy back. There's no longer anyone there telling you that you can't do something or putting you down for even trying. Sing in the shower. Blast your favorite music at home. Dance in your kitchen. (My son's friend Ryan told me last summer he's scarred for life after I was trying to do the "Flosser" while making dinner. That comment alone had me howling for 20 minutes.) So I guess I'll add dancing lessons to my list of new things to do.

CHAPTER 16

So Where Is God in All This?

God wants you to be delivered from what you have done and from what has been done to you—both are equally important to Him.

– Joyce Meyer,
Beauty for Ashes: Receiving Emotional Healing

As I floundered my way through my destructive marriage, I would often ask God, "Why?" Why was He allowing me to be abused? What was I supposed to learn? I even asked him repeatedly to show me a sign that it was time to leave. I literally even prayed for a billboard to pop up on I-35. It didn't, so I began to lean on Him more and more, and I heard God whisper to me, "I have you in the palm of my hand, Laura. Keep trusting in Me."

Christian friends or acquaintances would often say to me, "God doesn't like divorce." Well, I can tell you, too, that God doesn't want his sons and daughters to be abused, mentally or physically. Don't listen to judgment from others. When I realized this, I felt like a bird that had been given its wings. It was time to fly.

Leslie Vernick is a licensed clinical social worker and relationship coach. She has written several books on destructive relationships. Ms. Vernick says, "God's ideal for marriage still hasn't changed. He still wants it to be a lifetime relationship, but hard hearts still cause serious wounds to people and relationships. There are times it is just not wise or safe to stay married if the destructive person hasn't had a change of heart. They would have too much power to continue to hurt you."[39]

> Ephesians 5:25: Husbands, love your wives, just as Christ loved the church and gave himself up for her.[40]

I can tell you that my ex-husband, as you've realized throughout this book, didn't love me the way Christ loves the church. He didn't love me at all. Narcissists aren't capable of true, unconditional love. There are always strings attached.

It doesn't mean this divorce path was easy. But I can tell you, I am closer to the Lord than I ever thought possible. There is a sense of peace that comes with knowing God works all things for the good of those who love Him.

While I was in the firestorm, I began to serve my church in ways I hadn't before. I became an usher for the Saturday night services and during special events. I attended a Bible study for women near my home. I joined a divorce recovery group, and I now help with those same classes. I feel like God has shown me my purpose for this life He has given me: to help other women and men who are going through what I went through for decades.

I encourage you to get involved in your church. My sweet father often says, "There are good people at church."

I was having a bad day recently, and I opened my email, expecting more bad news. But there was an email from the pastor of Divorce Recovery asking me if I could help teach a class again. He also wanted to make sure my son and I were fully recuperated from the flu. It was comforting and reassuring that someone cared enough to check on us.

I also encourage you to listen to His word daily. I love the podcast app on my iPhone. I follow pastors Dharius Daniels, Ed Young, Joel Osteen, John Grey, Steven Furtick, and Bishop T.D. Jakes. I may be driving or running my 6-mile run, but their voices and the Word start my day off RIGHT. God has you where HE has you, and He will bring you through it. He will place the right people and messages in your life to steer you, but you do have to listen. To get to it, you've got to go through it.

Also, continue to pray, pray, pray. There is power in prayer. The morning of the important temporary orders court hearing, my dear friends Johnny and Allison gathered around me after our early morning workout. We held hands and I cried. We prayed for about 20 minutes. Just a few hours later, my attorney called and said my ex agreed to the temporary orders. I know God listens. He is there. Reach out to Him. Lean on Him. Let Him comfort you.

As I mentioned, one of my favorite pastors is Dharius Daniels, out of Change Church in New Jersey. I first heard him at my hometown church, Fellowship Church, in Grapevine, Texas. He was a guest of a huge church conference there called "C3." Pastor Daniels believes in changing your mindset to change you. He says you do this by filling your mind with positive thoughts and God's peace. Don't doubt your faith and God, but doubt your doubts.

Pastor Daniels recommended looking in the mirror every morning and saying, "I love me some Jesus and I love me some me." God and Pastor Daniels certainly don't want us to be vain. This is simply showing gratefulness and appreciation that God made you—YOU. You are special. You've been through so much. You deserve peace and happiness and joy.

> *Remember, you are special.*
> *You are strong. You've been*
> *through so much.*

My favorite sermon of all time is called "Forgiving Me" by Dharius Daniels. It's not easy being a single mom, but it's certainly not as toxic and debilitating as my marriage was. These points from "Forgiving Me" get me through the tough times:

1. Recognize that God is sovereign. We have power, but God is in control.

2. Realize you gain more from your losses.

3. Remember that you can't undo it. Regret doesn't make it better, it makes you worse. For you to recover, you can't be your best self if you are wallowing in regret.

4. Reflect on the fact it could've been worse. God loves you. There is mercy in this. It truly could've been worse.

5. Rejoice that God redeems time.

Point number five is my personal favorite. It's about forgiving yourself and your abuser. I should've left my abusive marriage years before I did. But I wasn't ready. Pastor Daniels reminds us that God is going to take the time you have left and make up for the time you have lost. It doesn't mean God is going to give you more time. It means that God is going to take the time left and He is going to blow your mind. God helps us catch up!

Remember, you are special. You are strong. You've been through so much. You have an army of men and women behind you, cheering you on, me included. Yes, it's hard. But you can do it. Keep fighting, pressing, and leaning forward. Your future is waiting…full of healing and happiness.

ACKNOWLEDGMENTS

This is the part of the book that is most difficult. There are so many people to thank.

First, I must thank God for bringing me this far. When I thought that I wasn't worthy of love and happiness, God encouraged me to press on. Don Ignacio at Fellowship Church: Thank you for being the worship leader who kept me focused on the bigger picture outside the pain. I won't pass the offering bucket twice, unless it's empty. I promise.

Also, I thank God daily for my post precious gift from all this: my son, Carson. I thank Him every day for the joy that child brings to my world. Carson is a mini Jerry Seinfeld and a Stef Curry wannabe, all rolled into one. If I need to laugh, my son provides the endless giggles to the point of tears. I love you, buddy. I love your joy, laughter, outlook on life, and the silly butt dance you do in the kitchen.

Thank you to my family. Mom, you did your best and we love you. May this book bring our family closer and repair the damage. My sweet Daddy, you are the best dad ever. I love you so much. May my future husband have all your qualities. And you're a pretty darn good Mayor, too. Thank you to my brother, his wife Crystal, and my three precious nieces and my one nephew, Dawson. You guys are the coolest kids I know. Caleigh, it's time for you to get a car. Aunt Laura approves. David, brother, we've grown closer in the last two years, I cherish us being siblings and close friends. You are a man of God, deserving of the beautiful life you've built. Aunt Lee, thank you for your love and support, and of course your canine expertise. I really appreciate you answering my calls when the puppy ate a light bulb. Aunt Lulie, thank you for being there through my divorce. You were my rock. I couldn't have done it without you. Uncle Charlie, one of the strongest men I know, thanks for your honesty after I made the decision to end my marriage. Your comments can't be printed here, but they made me laugh and yet see the truth in the situation.

Rebecca Lynn Pope: Words cannot capture the change you made in my life as a Life Coach and Spiritual Healer. Your encouragement, honesty (sometimes brutal), and humor makes every call with you something to look forward to. Your name is synonymous with growth, strength, and Godly love. Thank you. You will always be part of my tribe.

Ray Levy: You saved my life, literally, and your patience and knowledge got me through some of the hardest times in my forty-six years. I've known you for over half my life, so you cannot retire. You just can't.

Les Carter: Dr. Carter, I had no idea when I was calling on your clinic as a pharmaceutical rep in 2004 that our paths would cross again. Thanks for taking my call 13 years later! You have been a key part of the last eight months. I am honored to be promoting our books together. Thank you for sharing your expertise with me. Thank you for being my mentor, a Christian influence and most of all, my friend. Your patients are lucky to have you.

Chris Morrow: Thanks for the boat driving lessons and not throwing me overboard when I ran into the dock five times. Also, thanks for the graphics for the book. You are awesome and so are the graphics. When the lake crew convenes over the summer, the drinks and gasoline for the boat are on me.

Dennis Brewer: The Church is lucky to have you, but I am sure the women and men needing your divorce expertise are missing out. Thanks for being late for the 11 a.m. service to sit down and visit with me for the manuscript.

Holly Caplan: I am so glad our paths have crossed again, this time as single mothers and authors. You are amazing, and your book *Surviving the Dick Clique* is changing the way women excel in business. I think we need a board meeting at J Mack's.

Amy, Kim, Sunnie, Leah, Tricia, Andrea, Mandy, Pam and Shelby: The best girlfriends anyone could ask for. I love the laughter, trips to the beach, the pedicures and the boat rides. I welcome the issues we solve over wine or margaritas, because with you girls, we solve them every single time. I think we have an issue now that is up for discussion. See you tonight.

REFERENCES

1 *Why Does He Do That? Inside the Minds of Angry and Controlling Men*, by Lundy Bancroft (Berkley Books).

2 *The Diagnostic and Statistical Manual of Mental Disorders, Fourth Edition.*

3 *The Diagnostic and Statistical Manual of Mental Disorders, Fourth Edition*

4 "How to Tell a Sociopath from a Psychopath," Psychology Today.com, January 22, 2014.

5 *Healing from Hidden Abuse*, by Shannon Thomas, LCSW (MAST Publishing House).

6 "Love from the Perspective of a Narcissist," by Leif Beck. Soulspot.com, 10/2017.

7 Encyclopedia Britannica.com.

8 *The Diagnostic and Statistical Manual of Mental Disorders, Fourth Edition.*

9 National Institutes of Health, www. NIH.org.

10 National Institutes of Health, NIH.org, Stinson et al 2008.

11 "Meet the Real Narcissists (They're Not What You Think)," by Rebecca Webber. Psychologytoday.com, 09/05/2016.

12 "Love from the Perspective of a Narcissist," by Leif Beck. Soulspot.com, 10/2017.

13 "Love from the Perspective of a Narcissist," by Leif Beck. Soulspot.com, 10/2017.

14 *The Diagnostic and Statistical Manual of Mental Disorders, Fourth Edition.*

15 Psychologytoday.com, by Art Markman.

16 Dr. George.Simon.com.

17 *The Diagnostic and Statistical Manual of Mental Disorders, Fourth Edition.*

18 *Enough About You Let's Talk About Me*, by Les Carter, PhD. (Jossey-Bass).

19 *Enough About You Let's Talk About Me*, by Les Carter, PhD. (Jossey-Bass).

20 Per Dr. Les Carter; graphics by Chris Morrow.

21 *Corrections Compendium*, volume 35, issue 4, Winter 2010.

22 *The Empath's Survival Guide*, by Judith Orloff, M.D. (Book Depository International).

23 *Enough About You Let's Talk About Me*, by Les Carter, PhD. (Jossey-Bass).

24 *Enough About You Let's Talk About Me*, by Les Carter, PhD. (Jossey-Bass).

25 "A Field Guide to Narcissism," by Dr. Carl Vogel, psychologytoday.com, published January 1, 2006.

26 "The Narcissism Epidemic and What We Can Do About It," by Joe Pierre M.D. PsychologyToday.com, July 08, 2016.

27 *Why Does He Do That? Inside the Minds of Angry and Controlling Men*, by Lundy Bancroft. (Berkley Books).

28 *Why Does He Do That? Inside the Minds of Angry and Controlling Men*, by Lundy Bancroft. (Berkley Books).

29 *The Emotionally Destructive Marriage*, by Leslie Vernick, LCSW. (WaterBrook Press).

30 *How to Successfully Handle Gaslighters and Stop Psychologically Bullying*, by Dr. Preston Ni. Excerpts on psychologytoday.com, April 2017.

31 *Why Does He Do That? Inside the Minds of Angry and Controlling Men*, by Lundy Bancroft. (Berkley Books).

32 Centers for Disease Control, www.centersfordiseasecontrol.com.

33 *Will I Ever Be Good Enough?*, by Karol McBride, PhD, LCSW. (Atria Books).

34 *Will I Ever Be Good Enough?*, by Karol McBride, PhD, LCSW. (Atria Books).

35 The Anxiety and Depression Association of America, 2017.

36 The Anxiety and Depression Association of America, 2017.

37 Beyondthepurchase.org.

38 EMDRia.com.

39 *The Emotionally Destructive Marriage*, by Leslie Vernick, LCSW. (Water Brook Press).

40 Ephesians 5:25.

RESOURCES

Below is a list of resources to help you through your journey. I've listed videos, therapists, psychologists, websites, books and hotlines.

Books:
A Beautiful, Terrible Thing, by Jen Waite.
Enough About You Let's Talk About Me, by Les Carter, PhD.
Healing from Hidden Abuse, by Shannon Thomas, LCSW.
How to Act Right When Your Spouse Acts Wrong, by Leslie Vernick, LCSW.
Psychopath Free, by Jackson MacKenzie.
The Emotionally Destructive Marriage, by Leslie Vernick, LCSW.
When Pleasing You is Killing Me, by Les Carter, PhD.
Why Does He Do That? Inside the Minds of Angry and Controlling Men, by
    Lundy Bancroft.
Why Is It Always About You?, by Sandy Hotchkiss, LCSW.
Will I Ever Be Good Enough?, by Karol McBride, PhD, LCSW.

Podcasts:
Dharius Daniels, "Forgiving Me", November 29, 2016.
Steven Furtick, "It Can't End Like This", April 1, 2018.
Steven Furtick, "Never Not Enough", December 3, 2017.

YouTube:
Laura Charanza
Narcissism101; Dr. Les Carter and Laura Charanza
Rebecca Lynn Pope
T.D. Jakes: "Let Them Walk" Jan 31, 2017

Websites:
www.drlescarter.com

www.thehotline.org
www.lauracharanza.com
www.lundybancroft.com
www.marriagepath.com
www.narcissism101.net
www.rebeccalynnpope.com
www.thepopeagency.com
www.theuglylovebook.com

Twitter:
@drhenrycloud
@lauracharanza
@rebeccalynnpope
@uglylove7
@SouthlakeLCSW

Hotline:
National Domestic Violence Hotline: 1–800–799–7233

Email:
theuglylovebook@gmail.com